The phoenix within

Have you always felt like you didn't belong here c
like you were different from those you met in life
search for your own kind? If so read on... this boo
'The phoenix within' is the beginning of my spiritual journey, which started in
1996 with a dream about a stranger dressed in black, little did I know at the
time that thirteen years later, he was to open the door which leads me to
where I stand today. With my development from a soul rescuer, medium,
healer, psychic, teacher to facilitator of the sacred sound events this book also
includes lessons and tips to open your own psychic door way, and the first
steps to realising your highest potential,
'......Give your dreams wings, set them free....'

(From Raziels wish ...sacred sound)

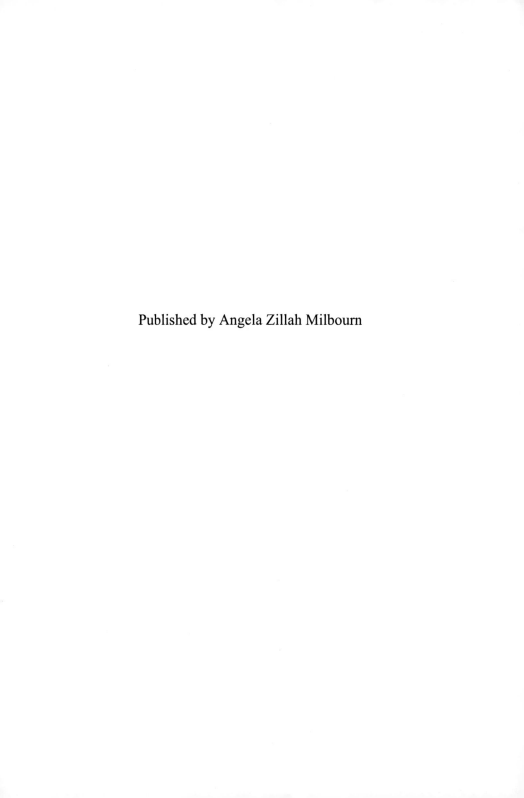

Published by Angela Zillah Milbourn

The phoenix within

The journey begins

By Angela Zillah

Aka angel shadow

Russell press

This edition published 2014

First published in 2014 by
www.russellpress.com www.russellpressdigital.co.uk

Copyright Angela Zillah Milbourn 2014
Angela Zillah milbourn has asserted her right to be identified as the author of this work in
accordance with the copyright, designs and patents Act 1988

ISBN
978-0-9930191-0-4

I dedicate this book
To Mary, Julie, Brenda and Tim for being
my guiding lights in my first steeps
And for all those who have walked with me
On this part of my journey
Namaste

Contents

'The Phoenix Within'
Foreword

'You should write a book!'

So many times I have been told this. My life has had its fair share of eventful happenings over the years to say the least. So here I am, after thinking I would write something that would sound like an entertaining and sensual Jilly Cooper novel. I find that what I am about to write is not about the life I had, but the life I now find myself living and the path that brought me to here.

There are thousands of books about the subject of spiritually and related topics, in all languages, faiths and beliefs, personal stories of spiritual journeys, and yes this is another, but this is mine, and I hope it is different.

However, within these pages there is guidance for your journey if you wish to accept it, as well as true stories.

I share laughter, tears of sorrow and joy, personal sadness which I removed before first editing, and was told to put them back in, and so it has also been painful in revisiting some of the negative experiences of my life, and this is not the focus of my book, however they too bring me to who and where I am here today, combined with, my experiences and the knowledge I have gained particularly during the past fifteen years.

I hope to assist you in increasing your understanding and awareness of the difficulties you may come across as you take your personal path of enlightenment. I hope as you end my book you will find something within its pages to ease your pathway and aid awareness using that which is useful to you as stepping stones for your life's journey.

In the early days of my spiritual growth, there were times that I was exhilarated, and other times I was terrified by the occurrences I had, like the appearance of beautiful beings akin to Jesus or angels, along with spectacular places with the brightest of light.

In these times you would have seen me with cascades of tears, streaming down my face, as I felt embraced by so much love and beauty.

There is no way I can describe or compare these events.

Then a hundred degrees, turn around, journeys to some of the very dark places I traveled though, where I was challenged by lower astral beings and places that are inhabited by dark entities.

These times you would see me with my heart beating so hard, I felt it would beat right out of my chest onto the floor in front of me, Leaving me completely shell shocked and questioning my existence, abilities and sanity.

Living this life can be so lonely, confusing and frightening; there is so much we just do not understand. Your sanity is always in question, by you as well as others.

You know as well as I do, some psychiatrists or close minded people quite easily explain, how different types of experiences are figments of our imagination, You are suffering from dilutions or maybe it's a result of childhood trauma or stress. Believe me I have questioned myself to the point of believing I should conform and contradict what I have experienced as many who know they are different from birth often do.

In truth there have been times when I thought I should have myself sectioned under the Mental Health Act. At the time of completing this book I am now fully qualified psychotherapeutic counselor, C.P.A.C.B . I.I.H.H.T. S.A.C.

W.S.A , added to my qualification's all gained in thirteen years, a late developer I may be, however it is never too late and we are always capable of far more than we believe ourselves to be, remember you are not what others say you are, reach out from the limitations people put on you, spread your wings and do not be afraid to fly.

I have brushed shoulders with excellent Psychotherapists who did not condemn me, why? Perhaps it is because in realty they may not truly understand me, and yet on some deeper level deep inside their heart, instinctively they know I'm not insane, and there is more to life than we know.

I can and have viewed this part of my life and the past that leads me to this point from an analyst and psychological perspective. I have pulled it to pieces, then put it back together again, to make sure that what I write, is fact not fantasy or that I live in some kind of fantasy world.

Although there are some critics that would say I do just that. Along with thousands of others people who are gifted with ability's and are of like mind like myself, all tarred with the same brush, and in days gone by would have been burnt at the stake or locked away, however, there has been too much evidence to suggest that the spiritual path I walk is due to some mental imbalance. I find I am well able to integrate both the mortal practical world and the world of spirit.

My psychological mindset sits quite easily in reality, plus relating directly to the training I did as a counselor, coupled with my own sensitivity that enhances my abilities with the work I do today.

When you first become aware that you are different, to the average Joe Blogs, you initially make a list of excuses to yourself to rule out the illogical parts of your experiences. You may find, when taking your first steps on the spiritual path, or even if you are already walking the path, the excuses you can make to yourself regarding your sanity, are endless;

I for one argued with myself for a really long time. In fact, until I was thirty eight years old.

There is no wonder, many of us do not say anything about what we see, feel, sense or hear.

We remain silent about the inner feelings and awareness that resonates within us, living in fear of ridicule.

However, times are changing, too many of us are now are singing the same song; to be branded as eccentric or insane.

Too many people now know there is more to life than this physical body we are in, there is much more to life than working, wanting material things and paying out for goods we actually do not need, they give use short term pleasure, and often a time comes when they don't mean as much as they did in the past

Your memories are in your head, and you may find yourself de cluttering your life, not just of material goods, but people too, don't feel bad about letting someone go, you are in fact giving them the wind beneath there wings to let them fly free again, if they should choose to do so, if they remain in their victim status or go back to where they were before you met them, then that is there choice, you are not responsible, for their actions they are, and you may find they blame everyone else for their negative life experience's rather than taking look at the part they played themselves and choosing to move forwards.

The spiritual pathway is not an easy one, it seems sometimes when things become too tough and your emotions are in total turmoil, it would be far easier to give it all up and live a material life.

You may be going through a number of bad patches and can't understand why times are so hard. You may feel you don't deserve all this crap that life throws at you and it is too difficult to cope with all the struggle and aggravation.

So many times I have heard students grumble,

'I'm leading a spiritual life I shouldn't have all this sh…'
Life is life, and sh.. happens.
So if you think being spiritual will stop it, think again.
If you think it will give you a fat bank balance and life will be
easy then you may be disappointed.
We are here to learn and grow, to move forward, into a new
higher level of understanding, and sense of awareness.
To raise our vibrational frequency to a higher plain of
existence, it may sound a bit far-fetched or a lot, depending on
your frame of mind, however by the end of my book you will
see where I am coming from, and I hope you will gain much
from the experience.

A good thing to remember is, some things are pre destined and
some are just simply life's rich patterns.
Take note that nothing is set in stone, as you will find as you
read the pages of this book.
Life is a fast moving board game, what happens, depends on a
mixture of, past conditioning, patterns, and themes in your
childhood, your character, your zodiac sign, destiny, luck,
karma, plus the life choices you make, the lessons you learn
along the way are just a few ingredients that makes up your
life's adventure.
Let's look at a simple example.
A Fortune Teller says to you, 'You will meet the man of your
dreams, have two children and live happily ever after'
A common scenario; so what happens if?
You are late to work that morning, miss your train and
consequently do not meet your handsome prince.
Or maybe you were on time, but he missed the train.
Perhaps you both had to catch different trains in order to meet.
The list of possibilities, are truly endless.

The spiritual path is not an easy one to follow, you have choices, it is down to you how much you allow it invade your life, and fill your life, a little, a lot, or now and again.

You may simply find you go to church once a week and that is all you need, or attend classes often or a little, to help you with your spiritual growth and understanding, you may have a topic you wish to learn more about, for example, I delivered angels, ascended masters, Sanskrit mantra, self-healing, spiritual and psychic development, shamanic drum, plus other sister classes that branch from these.

These classes in turn have changed and grown and include a new path of sound, light and sacred geometry.

Which are budding thoughts at the time of writing, my mind is flowing with seemingly endless new ideas.

The world of spirituality is vast and an almost endless list of options ways of working and growing, it may be you love fairy's, angels, dragons, runes, crystals, or alien forces, you may be a Christian, Buddhist, Pagan, Sharman Atheist, etc. The paths you can choose are too numerous to mention but find a path you will.

Atheist may sound an odd addition to the brief list, however much of what I teach now is and has been backed and proved by science, and it's not uncommon for atheists to be captivated by star wars and Jedi, or science fiction and they all have a related theme, a power force. Or as the phrase goes 'let the force be with you'

I say to my students, I simply give you keys to open doors, how many doors you open and which ones are your choices. Remember, the world of spirit will not force you to take a path you do not whole heartedly want, or need to follow, and when the going gets tough, you can give in and quit, or stick it out and watch everything eventually fall into place.

Believe me no matter how hard it gets, the rewards are far
more satisfying, the peace and inner knowledge and love you
gain from the universal life forces has no comparison.

Before we begin our journey together, a word of caution, as
you take your first steps or even if you are already wandering
along your spiritual; path, searching for the next piece in the
puzzle, like I did.
Don't let those that are from the pocket and not the heart fool
you into thinking you can have it all and have it now.
You will find people who will say they are better to train with
because they are more expensive, there courses are longer,
contain more case study, have more homework, you get more
material addition's for your money, they had more expensive
teachers, there mind may well be one of financial gain.
They may well be the best, but check them out first don't part
with your hard earned cash unless you're sure this is the right
teacher for you.
There is no fast track way to reach it, no matter what the
adverts claim.
No amount of money spent will make you superior to another
fellow workers, it is in essence from the heart; with love being
the key, yes there needs to be a form of exchange, for practices
and teaching to be respected after all you wouldn't expect a
therapeutic treatment or shop to give you everything for free.
Ask spirit to find you the right teachers, and don't rush of
spending your hard earned cash on every course or training that
you can find. Think about it, how does it feel in your heart?
Spiritual growth needs to come through devotion, control of
ego, love, patience, trust and faith, plus tolerance and
understanding of your fellow man.
Then the wider world of spirit will open up, but please
remember this takes varying degrees of time, depending on the
individual concerned.

I have found some people open up very quickly to the world of spirit. Some become frustrated that it's not happening quickly enough or they want it for the wrong reason, they may see what I teach is not for them, and go on to find some one more suited to their needs. And that is a good thing, its rules out something they know that they don't want, and so moving them a step into the direction they need to go.

I could tell you stories of what I have seen in my life time that would make a very good read. However, to say these things would be full of lies, sex, betrayal, deceit, material wants and needs, restricted development and ego, this might be a good read and perhaps a best seller. I have such a book in draft called L.S.D , which stands for lies, sex, and deception but it would not be of benefit to anyone who seeks spiritual growth, simply a knee trembling story full of gossip, and sensationalism
It is the past, and the past can only serve as lessons' to show us how far we have come.

Welcome to the new age!

'The time has come, the time is now'
(*From Tim Wheater's Heartland*)

<u>Introduction</u>

The Date is 11th June 2013, at last I find myself picking up a manuscript for a book; I started to write eleven years ago.

This manual has undergone first and second editing by friends, and now more words pour on to its pages, taking even more time

My urge to complete the books are strong, but like most people daily life often prevents one's personal quests from being followed.

So now spirit has put me in the position to write, and I must take great care not to let other practical household or should I say boat hold jobs take over.

As my life has brought me to living on a river on a narrow boat, something I would never have considered.

I found myself in a situation, I could find no solution to and with words of 'I can't carry on like this' and eyes cast upwards looking to spirit and the angelic realms for answers, six months later a solution to my problems appeared like magic.

I now find myself on a sixty foot narrow boat, bobbing about on the River Trent, for someone who had only been on a boat for a two hour pleasure trip under protest of, I didn't like water and I get sick on a garden swing, that's quite a challenge.

As I read the first few pages of the original manuscript, I am amazed at how much I have grown in such a short space of time, the words are simple and concise almost like a college essay.

I started my new spiritual life in 1998, and during fifteen years I have trained in a number of therapies and also become a psychotherapeutic counselor, something I never even expected. I have learned and grown beyond all my expectation.

So I will begin by thanking my tutors, peers, friends and my two Reiki Masters, Mary and Julie, for the first keys to open my doors, To Tim for throwing the first stone into my sound pond sixteen years ago, and to those sound teachers who have been an inspiration, to my friends who have edited and read this book, And those people who now enter my life as I walk a new path, to create sound healing vibrations so everyone can share its healing magic, and to the numerous spirit guides and helpers from many different realms who have shared this journey with me so far.

Many thanks from a humble heart.

I also now know, I'm not thick or stupid, a failure or insane, as I spent most of my life believing.

I am dyslexic; I had like many people issues of self-worth, low self-esteem and lacked confidence.

Just take a moment and ask yourself a question,

Do you become embarrassed or uncomfortable when someone says something positive or nice about you?

Perhaps underneath you feel pleased but on the surface you don't show it. If so you may have self-worth issues.

I started to write the 'The Phoenix Within' in the year 2002 and it is now in 2013, diary's and notes, as far back as 1998 when my wings began to unfold, come to life and remind me of how amazing the spiritual journey can be and how easy it is to forget those small miracles that happen every day, that get lost in living life.

I finally realise the early manuscript I read through is in fact the bare bones of my book and it is now time to put meat on those bones. Or cheese sauce on the cauliflower if you're a vegetarian.

As I write this book notes for the next books fall onto the paper, titles ring in my head, 'Phoenix in the Shadows'; 'Release Your Phoenix'; 'The Phoenix in Flight' 'Changing hats'

In between thoughts and ideas, spirit channels as I go to bed
a new book 'Phoenix visions and Dreams', notes pile up on
scraps of paper, jotters and even the backs of shopping receipts,
waiting to be brought alive by the computer.

2013 sees songs and music fill my mind, angelic and higher
order tones, shamanic chants, and songs of the 'Hearts notes'
full choirs and orchestra's play in my head. More scraps of
paper and snatches of tunes recorded on a dictaphone in case I
forget, And what's more I cannot write a single musical note.
How to make the new phase of my life happen is the question
poised on my lips, I can neither read music or play instruments
well, and so I wait on the will of heaven, knowing that spirit
will bring to me those I need, who will bring the music and
songs in my head alive, the P word champs at my heels,
'Patience dear little one' I hear them whisper in my ears.
Like a child full of excitement and yet the adult eagerness
presses those grown up response's, as I write my book within
my new home, aptly named River spirit, and that my friends is
a story's for
'The phoenix in flight' and 'Changing hats'
College ended for me almost three years ago, four and a half
years of counseling education has changed me in ways I never
expected, and if I can come this far on something I didn't
expect to last ten weeks, then anything is possible and here I
am positive proof.
I am no scholar, as no doubt my style of writing, grammar and
use of words will show. This book has not gone through a
publisher or agents hands, and so it is in a basic form.
However I write from the heart and soul, as this book is for
you, the reader!
It's personal, as though I am there with you in the same room,
sharing cups of tea, and short bread biscuits, sitting by an open

log fire in a candle lit room, incense drifts through the ether in curls of blue smoke, peaceful, calm with an air of anticipation.

As I prepare to tell you my story, a remarkable spiritual journey that will continue to unfold as the night draws on, it's a bit like a soap opera only this is not fiction it is real.

No doubt you may feel some of what you read cannot possibly be true, if so that's ok too, I hope that you will just enjoy the adventure.

If you are reading spiritual books, then you are searching for answers and you have already started to grow.

Your world which will unfold may not follow the same patterns as mine; nevertheless it will still be as fascinating and as individual as you are.

If my experiences can shed a little light on what is happening to you, or perhaps open a door to something better then I have achieved all that I could hope for.

'Remember that even the smallest thing you do to help the planet and her people, can make a big impact on others and make the world a better place.'

First Senses

I think a good place to start telling you my story would be with my early experiences of spirit. My involvement with their world, or should I say their connection with me, this includes the need for me to speak about some of the life experiences we all face during the journey that leads to personal awakening and a new kind of life.

I could never have imagined the journey I have had and continue to have. I will share with you some of the things I experienced in my earlier years of growth and give comparisons, and may be a taster of some of the things that you might experience on your spiritual journey.

Also integrated within the pages are some basic growth exercises. These will aid your spiritual development, even if you are mid flow leading a busy life.

As a child my gifts were not at the fore front, however my grandmother it seems was well aware I was different.

Unlike an acquaintance I once met, who told me that when he went to visit his grandmother, he was fastened to a table leg with a couple of ties end to end, and then they were tied securely around his middle, giving him minimum range to wander. He was then given a crystal ball and told to watch the pretty pictures, in order to stop him emptying her cupboards and getting into mischief.

The only confirmation I had to say I was different was my grandmother, who told me when I was young that we were of Romany ancestry. I had a gift that came with my name Zillah and that every youngest child's grandchild would carry the name, plus many stories of individuals in my Romany ancestry, I sadly cannot remember.

She would look at me deeply stroking my hair and would say, `you're mine, I know your mother had you but you are mine'

I never understood openly what she was saying to me at the time. However deep within my heart I knew, I was different in some way.

At an early age I sensed so much. I responded to this extra awareness as you would a passing thought and I paid little attention. Yet deep down, I knew that I was different to the other children that I knew.

I always felt like I didn't quite fit in, and I didn't belong here on earth even though, I was brought up in a loving family.

I was quite happy in my own company busying myself making things, and living in a play world with my unseen friends along with the children that no one else wanted to play with. They were labeled fat, ugly, thick and so on, by the more popular children, and bullying from them, was part of our daily lives.

In my young mind I often knew of events before they happened. I sensed people's thoughts and feelings; passing spirits were part of daily life. I saw them and talked to them in my head, and they would talk back, I saw them as clearly as I see them now.

As a child trips to stately homes and halls were frequent and I would enjoy wandering from room to room, sensing naturally which rooms would get a second visit; I wandered aimlessly around, my little body and mind buzzing, it all felt so good, I felt so at home, comfortable and very happy with the atmosphere generated by those, that were long gone.

It was as though something familiar had brushed by in my young life.

I would relish the thoughts of visits to stately homes, in particular Thorsby Hall in Nottinghamshire.

Which are now interestingly just a few miles as the crow flies from where I now lived as I write this book.

These days it is part of a hotel chain and health spa, although in my childhood days it was owned by the National Trust.

I loved walking around the hall, I can still recall the musty smell of the aging items, that filled the rooms, the dresses on manikins of people who had long since died, high beds with canopies, thick polished twisted bed posts, heavy dusty drapes, thread bare carpets, and furniture surrounded by thick red ropes on brass fitting to protect them from eager exploring hands.

I would marvel at the vast oak dining table, set for imaginary visitors with the finest china, and then watch the sunlight as it streamed through the windows making the crystal glasses sparkle like diamonds.

The old wooden floors were polished so intensely you could see your reflection, quite a contrast to the coldness of marble tiles and winding metal staircases, ancestors looking sternly down from huge paintings hanging high upon the walls, eyes watching every move and whispering shadows of days gone by.

Clocks that echoed through the halls, ticking the past and the present time away, each second a tick of life passing by.

I remember as I walked up the stairs of Thorsby Hall, a small dolls house type arrangement with stuffed mice in place of dolls, dressed as maids and the lord and lady of the manor in noble outfits. It always fascinated me and was one of the things I would have taken home.

I knew the place well and it always seemed to be quiet when we visited, unless I was just lost within my own world not registering people around me.

I would wander off enjoying every sense and smell, with my thoughts drifting into times past, giving me a buzz of excitement that never seems to leave you, when walking within the realms of spirit.

Some of the rooms I loved would get a second visit, nevertheless even at that young age, I sensed those that

alarmed me and I steered clear of them, on occasions
running past the doorways to these rooms as fast as my little
legs could carry me.

I recall one childhood experience of fear which overwhelmed
me, when we were on one of our family trips, this time to
Haddon Hall in Derbyshire.

On this particular visit my fear and tears were not without
reason, although I did not know at the time why.

This is the event as I remember.

My father was looking into a pond, in the grounds of the
Haddon Hall; I think it was at the back of the house.

He held my baby brother in his arms, as I went over to be with
them, I looked into the pool and became so alarmed, that I ran
back to my mother in tears and feared for my brother and
father's safety. At that time I did not know what had made me
so afraid.

However, ten years later in 1980 the reason for my fear came
to light.

At that time I was twenty years old and I was working at a
chocolate factory in York. Whilst there I met and became
friends with a lady called Valerie, the other women warned me
off her saying,

'Watch, that one… she's a bit eccentric, or a few bails short of
a full load so to speak.'

However I was drawn to her, I enjoyed and looked forward to
working with her. She had a nice smiley face, short dark
brown hair and pink cheeks. Valerie had a kindly look about
her, like you would imagine a friendly farmer's wife in
children's story book.

We had many interesting conversations while we packed
chocolates, and I learned that she wrote children's books in her
spare time and hoped one day they would be published.

I choose to work with her as often as I could. I found I trusted Valerie and I started telling her about my experiences as a child and what I was experiencing then in 1980.

Like my friend Mary who I had yet to meet some eighteen years later, Valerie would listen and talk quite openly about spirits. I was intrigued when she told me about her friend that would stroke sick animals and make them well. How she could tell things from holding an item that belonged to someone else, then relay information, to the enquirer about the owner of the item. I so wanted to meet this lady but it was never to be.

Little did I know that I would also be able to do such things, and later go on to teach others?

I told Valerie about the pond at Haddon Hall, and she responded by saying, 'Oh a monk was murdered there,' she said in a casual matter of fact way. So that was one mystery solved.

I had lengthy conversations with her about my senses and feelings; there were the place within the factory where I became afraid. She told me of the events that had taken place there in the past, and it came to light I was in fact picking up the residue of energy left by people's deaths and began to understand that I was different.

JETTA HOUSE 1973

Recalling the Meeting with Valerie leads me on to remember my experiences in my early teens.

By this time I had become well aware of my sensitivity and perception and able to use it to my advantage.

I wasn't in fact destined to meet Valerie from the chocolate factory for a further seven years.

I was thirteen years old, and by now my gifts had grown stronger, at this stage I was often able to know what someone was going to say before they spoke, I would see events before they happened and out of the corner of my eye, I would catch glimpses of figures passing by, along with movements, and sparks, I would turn to look in their direction only to see no one was there.

'It's your imagination' I would say to myself.

It wasn't logical to see things that were not there.

Little did I know this was the point where my logical mind and psychic mind, were beginning to have different points of view and where seeds were being planted for self-doubt that would, later in life cause me so much grief.

Deep down inside I knew these fleeting glimpses were not my imagination, and yet I continued to take it all in my stride, like a passing thought it just happened, I felt it was nothing special and just accepted what I saw and heard as a normal part of my life.

I instinctively knew I could say nothing about my experiences to anyone. I knew it was real, although I doubted anyone else would believe me, plus I didn't feel the need to tell anyone any way, it was all very matter of fact.

I didn't give it much status in my life or even class it as important, until at the age of fourteen when the hand of fate intervened and the following event took place.

❖

It was 1974 and my family moved to Jetta House in Norton- le-Clay, a small village near Dishforth, in North Yorkshire.

This is where I started to grasp the full meaning of my difference, and developed a new awareness of spirit energy and the effect they can have on our mortal lives, the anger sorrow and misfortune they can generate due to their own life experiences that they endured as mortals.

The course of events that led to us moving from town to country certainly seemed to be based on pre-destiny; if it was not it is very unlikely I would be telling you my story today. A year before we moved to Jetta House, when I was thirteen, my parents had decided we would emigrate to New Zealand for a better lifestyle for us all.

The prospects looked good for my father an experienced carpenter and joiner and my mother very academic. A job and house awaited for us there and most of our belongings were sold, flights were booked and our future was mapped out, everything then seemed rosy.

Then disaster stuck, or so we thought. A week before we were due to fly out the housing chain broke and the purchaser of our house had lost their buyer for their house.

Everything was put on hold until a new buyer came along for our home.

Three months after we should have moved to New Zealand a bad earth quake hit the island in Christchurch where we would have been living. That would have been a real disaster, the list of possible horror scenarios of what may have happened to us was endless.

I remember the shocked look, on my grandmother's face when the disaster was announced, her head turning away and reaching to hold someone's arm; she was never very keen on us going anyway, although she would never hold any of her children back.

We had a lucky escape and acknowledged that perhaps if we had gone we might not have been here today.

A few months later we went to visit the old couple at Jetta House who had lost their house sale and prevented them moving to our house previously, they were still very eager to buy our home in the town and being in their twilight years they now needed to be closer to the amenities that were not currently available to them in a remote village such as Norton-le-Clay, so we all made the trip view Jetta house.

It was at this visit that my heart did a summersault and my love affair with the countryside began.

I was totally bowled over by the open country side, cattle, sheep and horses in fields nearby.

Best of all I was experiencing this over a fence not from a train or car window everything felt so much bigger and alive.

I felt it was the most wonderful place in the entire world, I could ever be.

This was a total contrast to our home in the town, where there were lots of buildings and people, noise and bustle.

Since then my love for the countryside has never changed and my anxiety when I go to a town has grown to the point I can barely cross a road without feeling tense and to some degree scared.

Fortunately for me, my parents decided to buy the house and the elderly couple bought our house near Castleford.

Our new life in the countryside began in Norton–le-Clay; this small village had no more than two dozen houses with most of the village being owned by the crown and run by a Squire.

We were a mile from the nearest bus stop, with no footpaths; public services consisted of mobile butcher, mobile shop, and the fortnightly library van, so facilities were minimal, and this in its self-had a heartwarming appeal, even now I can see the friendly butcher bring mum the meat, he really did look like you would imagine a county butcher in a story book, jolly round red face, striped cotton butchers coat and apron with his wicker basket and a brisk, polite welcoming manor.

I can recall the sweet smell of the mobile shop, even the one who used to visit around estate were my grandmother lived seemed to have a similar sweet smell.

This small village in the middle of nowhere was quite a contrast to Leeds, where everything was on your doorstep or a few minutes bus ride away.

A place where the 'Barbour' jacket' and green wellies were unheard of.

So as you can imagine four 'townies' moving into a rural community was somewhat of a novelty for the local inhabitance.

Nevertheless we were still human and had to eat like everyone else, which meant a long walk to the nearest shop over a mile away to the 'Naffi' at R.A.F Dishforth.

Armed with shopping bags, mum and I would set off down the country lanes dressed in a suede mini-skirts, patent leather platform boots, and fun fur jackets; over roads little better than tracks, much to the regular amusement of the locals.

We would stager back under the weight of shopping bags, tottering on the platform soles.

(Needless to say even though platform shoes are back in fashion, I give my misshapen feet the comfort they deserve, My 'Barbour' jacket and green wellingtons are without a doubt an essential part of my wardrobe).

So under groaning shopping bags and feet screaming for freedom we would enter Jetta House.

As we entered I would feel something attach itself to my left shoulder.

My instincts told me it was a presence, how or why it attached itself to me I had no idea, I didn't give it any consideration, It simple felt as if someone was pressing against my shoulder, in a strange way I never noticed a weight and yet when it wasn't there I felt much lighter.

(I will explain this phenomenon later)

The entire time we lived at Jetta House we seemed to have nothing but bad luck, one bad patch followed another, it never seemed to let up, nothing ever went right for us and it felt like a dark shadow hung over us.

We had little history about Jetta House, however, there were stories of how two men had been working in the fields near the house on a tractor at the end of our garden, a plane from the Dishforth air base had difficulties and came down, the pilots ejected however the farmers were both killed.

There was another tale about a woman who was looking for someone, who had been killed in the war.

Our family had all been seeing shadows and we were aware of a lady in grey who walked down our hallway on occasions, none of us ever spoke very much about these experiences.

It was never said openly, we were living in a haunted house! In fact the true story behind the haunting never came to light whilst we were there, at the time we probably didn't even consider that they may have affected our mortal live.

Since then I have come across so many cases where people's lives have been affected in various ways by the spirits of the long since died.

Some haunting's span generations and affect family after family that live in the property's.

As the years passed at Jetta House, the daily spirit events were just that and we accepted them as anyone does, What else could we have done, there wasn't the new age movement as we have now, where help is on hand and the world of the unseen is believed and understood to a degree.

So now I will take you forwards to *1976*
I was now a young woman, and I started work two days after I
left school, working at the 'Three Arrows Hotel' in Borough
bridge, as a silver service waitress for a sixteen year old girl
who had lead a quiet life it most certainly was an education in
to the variety of people out there in the big wide world.
I learnt fast, made mistakes like all youngsters do, that age of
innocence soon becomes lost in such a colorful environment.
I had always been a hard worker, so long hours, and no buses,
often meant leaving home at half past five in the morning and
sometimes not getting home till one o'clock the following
morning.
I would walk to R.A.F. Dishforth to catch the first bus to
Borough Bridge, in all weathers, my love of the countryside
never waned as each morning I would wait at the corner of a
field.
I remember cool mornings with frost covered roads held
beneath the moonlight's gaze, dawn beginning to break
through the indigo of night, the silence melting away as the
dawn choirs of birdsong filled the air, announcing the arrival of
a new day, the rising sun making its appearance, kissing my
face with the first rays and feeling like had been blessed,
I don't really remember the bleakness of the winter times when
the cold wind, snow and ice must have blown across the open
fields, biting into my bones, or the rain soaking me through to
the skin, getting on a to the bus wet and cold.
I just loved the space and the quietness, the isolation, the
feeling that I was complete.

At the age of nineteen, on June 2nd 1979 I found myself
married in an unsuitable relationship; to a man called Mark that
I didn't even want to marry.
This is where thirty years later the understanding of self-worth
is clear.

However at the age of seventeen, I believed men were superior, and in order to prove myself I must be a good wife and mother. I had a dream of two children, a little house with dandelions around the door, to work and cook and clean and expected to be happy, it seems so innocent and childlike now.

I was a timid creature, I lacked confidence, I was so afraid of him, due to my inexperience, I believed mark must love me to want to marry me, however he had an ulterior motive, and when he discovered that I wasn't rich, he planned to make my life expectance somewhat shorter.

I met mark when I went out with my father to the local pub; we played darts, and dominos. I don't even remember our first date or anything of the early times, he asked me to marry him in the car, I said yes and duly went home announcing I was going to be a Mrs, and went to bed, He bought me my ring in Bridlington, in Yorkshire.

All I remember before we got married and after was physical, mental and sexual abuse. I remember my wedding day as though it was yesterday; the bridesmaid's car had a puncture. I could barely stand as I stood at the church door, the congregation waited for my arrival and as the organ played 'Here comes the bride' my knees buckled, beneath me, I did not want to marry him.

Why did I? You may be asking yourself at this point, well I didn't want to let everyone down, after all the expense and trouble, everyone had gone to, and so I went through with it as expected, In the years that followed, I feared for my life on many occasions, I accept full responsabilaty for my actions and choices.

In about 1980 my parents decided to sell Jetta House and my husband Mark and I went along to help them with the house move. I felt compelled to walk around Jetta House, alone for one last time to say goodbye, I didn't understand why, but it was an urge that was far too strong for me to ignore.

I stood in my parents' bedroom looking at the emptiness and remembering some of the experiences from the past, I moved to look out of the window over the green fields. Feelings of why I had left all this behind to live in a terraced Barrett house', with my violent bully of a husband, surrounded by people I did not really know. And who did not realise the cruelty that was inflicted on me behind our closed door.

I stood looking out over the fields. It was then I heard my first spirit voice, it said, 'Please don't leave me hear alone.'

I didn't feel shocked, surprised or afraid of anything, I just said, 'Ok, you can come with me but no more bad luck.'

My response was a natural one without thought or questions it just seemed normal. I simply reacted spontaneously giving it no more consideration.

I went outside and waited by the garden wall, while mum picked me some flowers.

She presented me with a large bunch of giant yellow chrysanthemums and handed them to me wrapped in newspaper. I love chrysanthemums so much and as I held them in my arms, at this point lost in my little world of smell and sight, unbeknown to me my spirit friend was also preparing to come with me.

We took mum and dad to their new house and returned to our own home, the illusion of a good husband and contented wife, vanished with the closing of the door.

Mark was on continental shifts and he went to bed, I pottered around making a reason to stay away from him, praying that it would not be demanded, that I joined him.

I placed the flowers in a vase, and felt a strong urge just to look at them. I sat in the armchair gazing at the beautiful, bright sunny flowers for ages, mesmerized by their delicate and yet large pompom heads, formed from a multitude of small curved petals each as perfect as the next, there distinctive perfume lingered in the air.

When all of a sudden my senses kicked in, and it was then I became aware that I was not alone in the room.

The atmosphere around me had changed, although at that time I could not explain how or what I felt, I just knew things were different. The spirit presence had in some way transported itself in the flowers those words of 'ok you can come with me but no bad luck' had been acted upon there was no thoughts of pending bad luck, how much worse could my life get, whoever it was, was there with me, it would know the truth and I was no longer alone.

It is the only time to date that I have come across a spirit entity attaching to cut flowers; However, I have come across a number of cases where they have been known to attach themselves to objects. On occasion, leaving the previous wearers impressions on the item, that can affect the new wearer. Elemental enteritis can attach themselves to trees and plants plus various other objects. I have had many a broken stem on my plants caused by a visiting elemental making their presence known whilst working with students.

When you sense feelings from items we call this psychometry. Going back to my friend Valarie, at the chocolate factory in 1980 she had a friend who sensed this residue energy enabling her to pick up information about previous wearers, something which I was to teach my students, twenty five years later.

Life's Lessons

Over the years that followed my marriage with mark was
difficult, bullying and abuse was part of my daily routine.
I found comfort with the spirit that now lived with me, that had
transported its self among the flowers from Jetta House to be
with me. I was now quite sure it tried to protect me the best it
could, I say this, because at that stage of my development I
could not sense the gender of spirit, I knew it attached to my
left shoulder, as it had done at Jetta house. I knew nothing of
'soul rescue' and 'medium-ship'.
As far as I was concerned it seemed that he or she was very
lonely and so was I all I had to give was love, and that is all it
seemed to need.
My marriage was an endless balancing act of trying to do the
right things and so avoid and limit the daily abuse, No one
knew about the attempts he had made to suffocate me or drag
me into a swollen river, hold knifes at my throat, to half
strangle me in jealous rage, thanks to his brothers intervention
on that occasion he released me.
His efforts to have me dead and for it to look like an accident,
was the result of him discovering I wasn't from a rich family.
He bought me a second-hand twin tub washing machine, telling
me, 'You have to take of the back and wiggle the wire to make
it work.'
Then he added, 'Oh, It leaks but don't worry about that, it's
just a bit of water' so, there I was stood in a pool of water
wiggling electric wires. Numerous electric shocks later, the
realisation dawned that he had hoped to gain from my death by
electrocution. Conversations about a new life policy which he
had taken out on me to the value of three quarters of a million
pounds, the wringing gesture on one occasion of his hands
eventually along with a range of other revelations, gave the
game away.

The penny dropped!

I had married him thinking he loved me, in my innocence I had sealed my own fate.

The night I found my strength and courage to stand up to Mark for the first time, he had hurt our dog, in his drunken state. Once more I faced his flick knife, however this time I came back at him with a barrage of angry words. I shouted and screamed at him with all the anger and venom of a viper. Words coming fourth that had been hiding within me spewed out like a larva rush. I did not care at what the outcome might be, even if it resulted in my death. I screamed predications at him foretelling his own death; He sat still in the chair before me in total surprise. I can't remember what happened next, or the days that followed, I had faced his flick knife without fear. And it is to the lonely spirit I owe more than just gratitude. It was my strength and I believed acted as a guardian angel.

From that point on my abilities took on a growth spurt, my senses were sharpening, I had sensed for some time he was having going to have an affair with my best friend, however, I didn't make any attempt to stop it .

The prediction I had screamed at Mark hit a cord somewhere within him and made him fearful for his own life, the boot was now firmly on his foot. My friend was by now openly his girlfriend, and he had told her what I had said, and so she had taken the flick knife and broken it into a number of pieces and placed it in dust bins around the estate, so that it could never surface again.

I did experience all the feelings of rejection, even though it gave me a sense of freedom and a view to an ending of my marriage, as there love affair was quite open, and here I was in a surreal situation with the two people who were supposed to care about me, his sexual antics described to me in detail and comparing me at every turn, and now a new kind of cruelty came into play, I was nothing, worthless, pathetic, he then

decided he would become Mormon, so he could openly keep
us both, my position was to cook, clean, carry out house hold
chores and go to work, while she took on other duty's.
It still hurt and I had no one to blame but myself, in among all
of this, their relationship gave me the gate way to freedom.
Everyone could see this happening; they did not see the events
behind closed door.
I'm sure my lonely spirit cared for me, giving me strength and
insight, and saved my life many times during the marriage.
I guess I can now say it was my first 'Spirit Guardian'.
I'm sure if it wasn't for my spirit friend I wouldn't be here
today so wherever you are, I thank you with all my heart.

Eventually sometime later, I instinctively knew that my spirit
friend needed to be set free. Whether it was a case of instinct or
an inner knowledge, I didn't really know.
One night I lay in my bed, the dust had settled and I was
waiting to move out of the marital home.
My spirit friend always slept by my right side and by now I
could as sense it presence larger and more solid.
I spoke to it as I always did, but this night was different I said,
'It's alright; you can go now … I'm ok.' I remember the
feelings of love and gentleness
There was no big ceremony, no opening of energy portal or
doorways to the light, I simply said I was ok and in doing so
gave it permission to leave, I reassured it several times and
gave it thanks for all it had done for me, I just felt love and
gratitude, the next morning I woke up and it had gone.
My spirit friend's job was complete; weather it was planned by
the world of spirit or we just found each other I could not say,
however I did feel it needed to be loved. It was some years
later I learnt that you sometimes need to give a spirit
permission to leave, by giving reassurance, and then letting
them go.

In my book 'Release your phoenix' I will introduce you to some ways to help to rescue and release normal earth bound spirits.

Eventually over the years I learnt to apply reasoning and support, to the dead, as naturally as I had formed a friendship with the lone spirit, I found myself counseling the dead, the same way as I do the living.

With my spirit friend gone, I was in the process of Mark becoming an x husband; his love affair ended however he never did her any harm, and only showed her kindness.

This compounded my self- worth belief, I must be deserving of the treatment I had received from Mark.

Jacobean inn

After I had left the marital home, I found lodgings in a
sixteenth century inn, in small village on the out skirts of York
called Wiggington.
Mark remained in the house until it was sold, and as the
mortgage was in both our names I was entitled to half of the
house sale, of which I wouldn't have had, if he had been
successful in his next plan. Mark stated we would see a
solicitor of his choice together and all bills until the house was
sold, where to be taken from my share of the house sale.
However he didn't bank on the solicitor we were allocated
within the solicitors group, been a female, who was very aware
that all was not as it seemed and that I was just agreeing out of
fear. She did make sure I got the full balance that I was entitled
too, and Mark did not challenge her.

Freedom is far more important than belongings, and to wake up
in the morning unafraid of the day's events ahead was a
beautiful thing to have.
I moved to the inn with a second hand fold up bicycle, which I
had been given as a means of transport, as once again I found
myself with a long walk and no busses to get me to work.
The fold up bicycle had a mind of its own and attempted to
fold its self-up while been ridden, and then refused to unfold
when you wanted to ride it.
I had a few meager possessions and a kettle. Living on
whatever could be made with boiling water, instant mash
potato, gravy or custard, a boiled egg you would be surprised
what you can do with a kettle of hot water.
I was almost twenty two years old, having rented a room from
the owners of the inn and later going on to work for them.

Soon discovering I had a flare for the license trade, and since then I have spent many years of my life working behind public bars in restaurants and managing them.

It was about this time I was becoming more aware of energies and spirit presences. My ability to know what people were thinking was still very strong within me, this was something I was aware of from the age of thirteen, as I grew into adulthood, when I sensed that someone was thinking something wrong about me, I would create a situation so I could say what I wanted to say, changing their initial thoughts about me if it was unfair or wrong.
A confused look often resulted on their faces as if to say
'How the hell did she know I was thinking that?'

The inn had its fair share of ghostly apparitions, along with a number of power cuts, And so it wasn't unusual in the eerie atmosphere of a sixteenth century Jacobean setting, bathed in flickering candle light with low beamed ceilings, creaking doors and crackling log fires, for me to spin a ghostly tail or two to entertain the customers. On a number of occasions this saw the toughest of men building up the courage, walking almost hand in hand, with the bravest of the group heading the expedition, to the gents 'Toilet'
Then hearing a stamped as the heroes ran back down the passage way from their adventure, eager to reach the bar, as fun and laughter took over, leaving the last expedition member alone in the darkness, more than likely urinating down his own leg in an attempt not to be left behind.
They would burst through the door laughing, at their friend who had been unfortunate enough to be the last man, you would hear him hurrying to the bar door and then his last few foots steeps slow, walking in casually as if to say he wasn't scared at all. However they never went to the toilet alone.

Many who came were quite uneasy in this old Jacobean inn, who, if those walls could talk what tails they could tell.

The only time I felt uneasy within the inn walls, was some time after I started working there on a Sunday night, when my whole body was uneasy, an air of fear lay in the flickering shadows, filling me up like liquid lead, those final words of 'Good night….' as the last customer left for home, and it was time for me to lock up the bar, I would try not to show the shadows I was in fact afraid, and I had implemented a practice to help me with my own fear, yet I doubt that I fooled what ever made me afraid.

I begin by propping open the bar door with a stool, so the passage lights would still shine into the bar area, then I would turn off the bar lights and run like a scolded cat out of the bar almost knocking over the stool and locking the door as quickly as I could behind me, I had on a number of occasions knocked over the stool in my haste leaving myself in the darkness and fumbling to get out of the bar.

I tried so hard not to be afraid even trying to slow my pace, acting almost as brave as the toilet expedition leader.

However, fear always got the better of me, and I'll admit to you I can run a lot faster scared than I can brave.

I never understood what I was afraid of, and to this day I don't know why, the only link I had was the energy I felt from a large pair of blacksmiths bellows almost as tall as I am, that were wedged in the alcove on the wall in the fireplace.

I had felt a strong sense of a child's presence about seven years old,, I saw fire and flame and herd the huff and puff of the bellows in my head, but nothing more, and nothing actually happened,

Whatever I was sensing at the time was enough to make me feel there was no way I would stay in the bar on a Sunday night on my own, not even if I was paid to.

Perhaps one day I will go and visit the inn and see what it was that frightened me so much. As I now interact with many kinds of dimensional spirit work.

As time moved on I felt spirit presences drifting around my daily life. I paid little attention. I was only twenty two years old, when a well-known brewery chain offered me my own public house. However cupid's arrow had pierced my heart, love walked in the door and sense flew out of the window once again. I turned the offer down of the public house, and followed my heart.

This relationship brought me down to the village of Upton near Southwell and I settled in my new home with James, on the outskirts of the village of Bathley, near Newark in Nottinghamshire.

It was a tiny cottage high on a hill, with door to door mice, who when you put them out side were back in the house before we were, no central heating, frost on the inside of the window's, tatty furnishings, and view like I had never experienced before looking out over fields, spanning to the next village called Norwell a couple of miles away, love had truly gripped me not just of James, but this little cottage. I thought I had it all, at last the dream a little house, dandelions around the door, my first baby growing inside me after eighteen months of trying, and a man who loved me.

However rose colored spectacles have a limited life time and as cupids arrow bends a bit as reality of the life you are living becomes clear, six years down the line I found my second relationship failing fast, this time it was, alcohol, public houses and James conditioned, drinking habits taking its toll on our relationship.

Once again I was too timid to stand up for myself and complain.

When I finally found the courage to stand up for myself, it was too late and I slipped into the brandy bottle to help me cope, for the first time. As the saying used to go 'If you can't beat them join them,' so I tried. I had never been a real drinker or smoker, James called me his doll.

I always had a gentle nature, often I thought I was cowardly in some aspects; I always did what was expected of me and whatever necessary to keep the peace, drifting along, and muddling through each day as it came.

Seeking peace at any price and putting my sanity and health at risk. They say the phrase 'if you can't beat then join them' not something I would ever recommended, I was in an environment where life revolved around alcohol and the opening times of the local pubs, a stock of alcohol always in the house, a constant stream of people drunk and in party animal mood. I didn't work at this point, I was told be the little women at home cared for by her man, bring up children , keeping house and still trying to be the perfect wife and mother and make my man proud of me, which he was and I was loved. And yet alcohol changes people, they don't see the embarrassment the mess, the difficulties they cause, the impact on the children, and alcohol kills love just as fast as physical abuse. I was already damaged in a much deeper way than I understood at the time, and this also added to the relationship difficulties.

Twice in my life when I was faced with my greatest relationship difficulties, there was only one place thought I could find peace, and that was in the bottom of a brandy bottle, I'm the sort of person who can get drunk on a pint, pregnant on a pint and a half and not remember a thing about it.

So well hidden was my secret drinking no one even
suspected, or perhaps they were either too polite to say so, or
maybe I was just too good an actress.

As things became unbearable I slipped further into the brandy
bottle, alcohol made reality seem distant, so I could pretend
everything was ok. I drank on the sly; a mug of innocent coke
cola looks no different when it hides a large amount of vodka
or brandy within its bubbles, I didn't like the taste, or smell,
I did like the fact it made me numb to the reality of another
failing relationship. Functioning like a robot under control even
with alcohol inside me my priority always that the children
were safe.

I did not know that the series of relationship events so far
compounded my self-worth, into believing it must be me I'm
doing something wrong; I deserve this for some reason.

A time came when I could pretend no more; I had actually
realised sometime earlier, to join them wasn't one of my
brightest ideas.

I stopped drinking instantly, and sank into a deep robotic
depression; and my personal deep seated issue that caused
other difficulties was also taking its toll.

At that point I found myself six months pregnant, with two
children and no money. I had nowhere to go and my future
prospects looked very bleak, No one would give me a break,
even though I was working full-time in a public house much to
the disapproval of James, and that in its self-extended the
relationship as work became my sanctuary. I needed a place of
my own for me and the children, I had just enough money
coming in, to take care of us, never the less a pregnant women
with two children, was not a landlords choice when it comes to
been a tenant. I carried on from day to day not knowing what to
do, I felt very alone.

It was then the unexpected happened and on a antenatal check
things were not as they should have been, the midwife said the

scanner was faulty, I knew she was lying, and I was sent to hospital for a check, my baby son had died, and in normal circumstance the placenta breaks and the mother becomes unconscious, I would have been in a dangerous situation. He had died a few weeks previous, however I just kept carrying him, I didn't take the hospitals advice to stay and be induced immediately. I went home sorted out my other children's care for the next day.

I calmly prepared myself for the next morning, when I would be induced. So with empty arms and a broken relationship I was back to the beginning.

I wasn't very knowledgeable about death, and although my son was dead when he was born, I knew he must be baptized.
A priest came reluctantly, at about eleven fifteen at night.
He seemed not to understand why I wanted my dead son baptized and accused me of having an abortion.
I knew instinctively that by having him baptized I was giving the soul of my son a chance to return from where he came; there had been some unusual spirit activity when I found out I was pregnant, although I do know now it makes no difference whether a child is baptized or not a soul, is a soul and will return from where they came.
The spiritual event surrounding my son Thomas's conception made me very sure he must be baptized. No one had told me this, at the time, I just knew it as a fact and he must be baptized in this case for him to return.
I had long since realised that when I looked into a new babies eyes I could see the old soul looking out, often the baby would be in some distress, and I would reassure the child everything was alright, and that they were safe. When the child reached

six weeks old, the old soul has forgotten the past life and then settles down into its new life.

My belief was confirmed in a book many years later, nowadays more and more special children are being born.

And here I will interject a short but vital message after hearing of a medium who told a couple who were trying for a baby, that their child was a crystal child, and another unprofessional medium adding her thoughts that there child would be autistic, because it was a crystal child.

That's absolute rubbish not all special children are autistic, it made me cross to think of the damage the medium had done to a young couple who were just enjoying the thoughts of starting a family.

Since 2010 I have started meeting babies who don't lose the old soul within the first six weeks of life, they are well aware of my energy's and the communication that takes place between us. These babies' are normally, of higher spiritual standing and have incarnated on the earth plane for a special purpose.

On a brighter note spirits of lost children continue to grow in the afterlife, whatever you believe it to be. My son is called Thomas, and it is no by grammatical error I say this.

A few years ago, Thomas came to my bed side late one night, I was surprised to see him he had never been before, He was a young man twenty one years old, I babbled a bit and said I was sorry I lost him, he smiled and reassured me, he had come to tell me he would look after his little brother and I wasn't to worry, Thomas teenager brother was going through some wilder behavior, free running up buildings, and well doing the rights of passage things that teenagers do, I had lost one son and it was hard as a mother to allow my second son to be free. Thomas does watch over his little brother still, and I laugh to myself as Thomas in this world will have to look up to his little brother literally as he stands six foot eight tall and has size nineteen feet.

Over my passing years, psychic events were many, they were part of my daily life and I said nothing to anyone about my growing awareness. I would watch the evening news, seeing such things as a train crash, killing many people going to work, in China. I had actually seen the event four days previous. 'Why was I seeing things I could not do anything about? It didn't make any sense to me.

At this point I started to think perhaps I was mad, but in my heart I knew I wasn't.

My second relationship had come to an end, but my spiritual development had not, and I was been moved forward to the path I am on now, although at the time I didn't have any clue. The next stage of my development saw me seeing shadows of people; I could tell you whether they were male, female, child, dog etc. I would see a shadow and then a person of the gender I saw would die three days later. I saw three shadows in one week and three people died in the village.

At this time I found myself in relationship number three failing once again and back to where I started; still searching for the dream, two point five children. Dandelions, around my door and waiting for my handsome prince who would treat me with the love and kindness my heart so yearned for.

On the other hand, this time the end result was the awakening of my spiritual self, and the start of the most incredible journey as well as changes within my life that I couldn't have ever dreamed about.

<u>The Great Escape</u>

In 1996, I found myself for many months packing boxes in
secret, changing personal ornaments and keepsakes of my own,
stock piling food, hiding anything that would not be missed.
Once again I had no money and nowhere to go, but my actions
made me feel nearer to freedom. Relationship number three
proved no better than relationship number two, and the lights in
my life were the children.

I was in robot mode and the brandy bottle sat under the sink in
among the washing up liquid and cleaners for a second time.
Life was hard, which I didn't mind physically however
mentally it was too much. I was very, very disillusioned and un
happy. Within this more deep rooted and compounded self-
worth issues, bringing me to the conclusion not only was I
insane, I deserved the negative treatment towards me I had to
be a bad worthless person.

Now life has a way of bringing those you need into your life,
when the time is right, and it just so happens that in 1997 life
brought Mary to me. Sixteen years after I had met Valerie in
1980 from the chocolate factory when I was twenty.

I had waited so long time for someone special to come into my
life who I felt would understand what I was, I didn't realise at
the time how meeting Mary would lead me to the first door that
would open and change my life and future path so completely.
This is how it all began for me, an introduction to the world of
new age practices and beliefs a true 'Pandora's Box'. Full of
all sorts of experiences and knowledge, leading to growth in a
way I could never have expected.

I told you of some of the sadder events in my life not to instill
any emotions of sorrow, or pity life is life we are here to learn

and grow, and as I realised my relationships had a pattern
and theme, and I didn't need to be in a relationship in order to
be successful or complete. I said in the introduction I did
remove the personal relationship part of my life, and I was told
some needed to be with in the book to demonstrate how, far
you can come. And at which point
'The phoenix within' had been freed,

Meeting Mary the first keys

One evening my daughter asked if her new friend Karen could come round to our house to play, I rang and asked Karen's mum to ask, if this was ok, 'Yes' she replied, and then she asked if she could come round too. I thought this is a little strange I didn't know her very well, but said it was fine to come along anyway. When they arrived the girls shut themselves away in the living room, Mary and I sat in the kitchen.

Mary soon became aware that I was in a lot of pain with a shoulder injury I'd had since I was at school and she offered to help. She explained she did Reiki and massage; it was a relief to think that the pain might stop even just for a little while. The shoulder had bothered me since I was fourteen years old and now at thirty seven and I hoped I was to get some relief. As she worked on my shoulder, she told me all about Reiki energy. It seemed too good to be true, a universal energy we can all tap into, that can heal body, mind and soul for your highest good I must admit I was very skeptical and didn't understand.

I then to my own surprise, found myself pouring out everything to Mary, telling her about the voices, shadows, and my experiences. This was the first time I had spoken openly about the spirits. I just let it all out; I had no fear of ridicule or accusations of madness.

To my amazement she knew exactly what I was talking about. Mary said, 'Yes I have a book about that' and she offered me the loan of it. I must have had a mouth as wide as a bucket, my head fizzed with excitement; my mind wanted so much to know more. She told me that the shadows I saw before death were of a lower vibration and if I had Reiki I would see nice things too.

I didn't know what she meant, but I was willing to trust, and what's more she was going to lend me a book, that would tell me more about people like me, I was so excited, I wasn't mad after all; I was like a dog with ten tails.

Now even though seventeen years have passed by and as a Reiki Master, the power of Reiki never ceases to amaze me. I use a number of energy's now as instructed by spirit. I am honored and humbled to be used in its service.

It was sometime before I saw Mary again, she had loaned me the book as promised, and my eager little hands could not wait to read it. It was called, 'Into the Light' by Lillian Beck I read it from cover to cover so many times.

There among its well-worn pages was one paragraph about people like me. It went along the lines of, 'These people are rarely able to handle it and become unstable.....'

I didn't care; unstable or not, at last there was confirmation that there were people like me, and now this left me with another question. 'Where are those people like me?' Unstable or not! I felt so pleased I was not alone after all, and I began to realise, I wasn't mad either.

Seven years later into my development, the book found its way back to me. I have since read it from cover to cover, many times, I planned to quote the passage that gave me the belief that I was not alone and there were others like me, for you, I've lost count of the times I read it to find it so I could quote it to you, but I cannot find it so perhaps you need to read the book yourself.

I also realised on its return to my hands, it was a self-help book explaining Chakras, auras and energies etc, and other ranges of knowledge. All of which I learned to use and work with over the following seven years. Yet I remember the first times I had read the book the content of its pages went straight over my head, and meant nothing to me.

I had however, clung to that small paragraph; in the hope that there were others like me, that was all that mattered.

This little bit of knowledge settled in my mind along with some very special dreams.

I had hope and that is a powerful force on its own to keep us going. Hope I would meet someone like me; hope I would escape and hope in some very unusual dreams.

I continued to work as mum, wife, shepherdess, builder's labourer, plus running a home and be my husband's business secretary. As well as tending the animals, two horses and a number of mixed live stock on the farm; plus working full time in a bar and restaurant. In those days I ran around just like a clockwork mouse, in the direction I was told to, or had to.

Dawning of the awakening

It was spring time 1998, a time of new beginnings; new cycles, death and decay of autumn and winter, gave way to new growth, spring grass poked itself through wind torn winter tussocks, and the lambing season had begun, the rounds of checking stock and the extra work of lambing, and at least a half dozen of extra mouths to feed at the farm, of orphans or unloved lambs, sometimes they would drop to the frozen or cold ground and mother wasn't able to revive them or if she was giving birth to more than one she wouldn't bother with the first one until the others were born, colder nights saw me taking these tiny little creatures' feeding them a mixture of brandy, milk and glucose, then wrapping them up in a wooly jumper, I suspended a fire guard over two hard backed chairs and placed an electric convector heater on the floor beneath the fire guard then I would lay the little lamb in the guard, sitting close by and turning them every five minutes or so.
Mucus would poor from there little noses and within a couple of hours bleats for mother filled the room at which point if mother was alive I would return her lamb who was more than ready to have a second chance, on one occasion a weak little lamb seam to stand no chance its half dead cold body hung in my hand, I had no brandy but after adding a large dose of whisky to the mixture a couple of hours later the magical bleat filled the house, I took him back to his mother, and put him down, at which he tottered somewhat unsteady, not due to the fact he had looked death in the face, but he had too much whisky and was drunk, managing two legs when you have a had a few too many is hard, enough can you imagine what it's like with four legs.

So onto the ending of the old life and beginning of the first steps to the new life,

My normal morning routines began with getting the children off to school and then start the rounds of feeding the livestock before going to work. I loaded the van with hay and grain, and then began my regular morning rounds; all this before going to my work at ten o'clock in the morning. I drove to the sheep field, and parked across the road opposite the gateway, it was too muddy to get the escort van in and out of the field; it was a difficult task as the field is also situated on a series of blind bends, so vision is very limited. I started to unload the grain and bales of hay, relying on my senses of hearing, as I ferried the food across the road and into the gate way.

A flock of beady eyes and hungry bellies greeted me with their usual throng of bleats. I climbed over the gate into the field, and began to feed sheep, trying to race them to the troughs, to pour the grain in, before I was stampeded and grain would go every were but the troughs, often ending up on the ground trodden in by frantic hooves, and picked out by the birds later. There was one clever sheep, who had been around for a few years, and also taught others she had a special skill, and had developed a knack of, slipping her head through the bucket handle as I poured the grain out, then lifting her head, making a run as fast as Stevenson's Rocket, with the bucket around her neck; desperately trying to keep the remaining grain to herself. This signaled to the others she's got more than the rest, a chase began, Mrs. Clever sheep, followed by more sheep in hot pursuit of the bucket, a free for all would break out each head butting the other out of the way until the bucket lay empty on the ground.

A lone sheep feeling pleased with its triumph would lick out the bucket a number of times, just in case a small morsel had by some miracle been missed. I walked back to the gate, to retrieve the bales of hay, and began to climb over the metal gate, with a leg either side of the bars.

I turned to look down the hill; I could see a green and white
lorry thundering round the bends.

Then climbing down, reaching for the remaining bale of hay,
taking a hold of the nylon bailing string, in preparation to
heave the hay over the gate the string biting into the folds in
my fingers as normal, feeling an instant sensation like a lead
weight bearing down on me, Shadowed by a deep sense of
unhappiness immediately, swallowing me up in a dark cavern
of despair. I was just doing what had to be done, like a
clockwork mouse. As I began to lift the bail, and struggle to the
gate, I could see the lorry starting its assent up the hill and into
the first series of sharp corners.

'I've had enough,' I thought to myself.

I placed the hay on the ground, and turned to the entrance of
the field, a blind entrance, knowing full well the lorry driver
could not see me; he would be traveling at about forty miles an
hour or more. He wouldn't know what had happened until it
was too late, flashed through my mind with calm and clear
logic, I waited those few final seconds preparing to step out in
front of the lorry, done gone.

As I was about to take my last and final step, a dark shadow
descended before me, it over shadowed me in height and width,
bigger than the ones I had seen before people died and now it
was my turn, I wasn't afraid, I only felt calm and accepting.
This shadowy intervention paused, me for only a moment, and
yet long enough for the lorry to pass by, only inches from me, I
can still feel the rush of air as the lorry passed and hear the
noise and see the pressure on my clothes as they were blown
back towards me. The driver sped along unaware that he had
almost become involved in a suicide; that would have looked
like an accident.

I stepped back from the entrance, my mind in a whirling daze,
stepping back towards the gate I sat down on the hay bale,
sharp dried grass and stems poking through the fabric of my

trousers, sharp stabs of discomfort, bringing me back to my senses. I realised what I had almost succeeded in doing, feelings of disbelief at my actions, fleeting moments of regret at being unsuccessful and in awe of the shadowy spirit that had stopped me.

I was overwhelmed with sadness; tears filled me to the brim, I sat on the bale of hay and cried, my thoughts turned to my children, my family, and the lorry driver and the impact I would have had on his life. The heartache, disruption and stress would I have caused him, my children being left with no mother, and my own family the loss for my four year old son and twelve year old daughter. I had never had thoughts of suicide before; it was an instant decision, and almost a fatal one.

Gathering myself together, I knew I had to go to work, I had the preparation for lunch time service, at the local public house that I worked at, children to collect off the school bus, tea to make, back to work with children in tow, get them fed and ready to bed tuck them in, sheep needed checking and feeding, horses, dogs, cats, goat, and hens to feed and bed down for the night, my husband's tea, do the paperwork, wash up just another normal day.....and to add to that list, I knew I needed also to prepare to leave my husband, another repeat pattern.

I felt I would be seen as a failure, nevertheless I had tried so hard this time and stayed within this relationship, for so many reasons making excuse after excuse to stay and work at this marriage, this life of empty, loveless and lonely exhausting drudgery, I was only fooling myself, and if I am honest I knew from my day of my engagement I was making an error, however I wanted the dream of those dandelion's around the door so much, I had nothing else to turn to, know where to go, and in my mind no option, once again doing whatever was needed to please others, I now know it was about self-worth.

What I believed I should be, what I thought others expected
me to be, we call this in counseling terms positive strokes.
Now I had been driven to the point of suicide;
I had to change my life, but how?

Later that week I went to see Mary, and before long told her
about my attempted suicide and the shadow that saved me. She
listened intently, she didn't pass judgment she just listened, and
handed me a picture of Mother Meera an Indian Avatar, along
with a mixture of Bach Flower remedies, to help me through
this distressing time in my life.
I still understood so little but on the other hand I felt I could
trust in Mary. I knew very little about her and yet I felt a deep
inexplicable connection with her. I had not fared well with
men, in my life and I certainly didn't feel I could talk to God or
Jesus, as I felt unworthy; so the female energy of Mother
Meera was right for me.
I carried the photo copy of her everywhere and slept with it
under my pillow at night. I would pray to her and ask for help.
Mary had told me to think about her and put my hands on the
picture. I placed my hands upon the picture and connected with
her energy's, having a warm feeling embrace me.
At that point I didn't understand the world of energy.
Although I knew I received great comfort from Mother Meera
and on occasions, I could hear her talking to me.
The following June, Mary gave me my Reiki One as a gift, and
from then on my life began to change very rapidly.

The Awakening

Part of my late afternoon routine in the height of summer was to check all the sheep to see they were all well and all accounted for, anyone of you who have kept sheep will know that they have the innate trait that if their head goes through something their bodies can follow; so chasing sheep from one field to the other is quite a normal event, for a shepherdess in the countryside.

Thankfully everyone was happily munching at the grass in the late evening sun, I not wanting to go home, at this point had taken to walking to the bottom of the field to sit by the stream, for a short while drinking in the peace and quiet listening to the bird song, the time and space a retreat I had created for myself, although brief, it felt so good.

The familiar connection with nature soaked into me, that wonderment from when I was fourteen, the love the passion, I had lost it somewhere along the way without even knowing, it became part of the drudgery of life, cold biting winds, frozen taps, long hard hay making and shearing of sheep by hand, knotted electric fences and walking miles to round up straying sheep, Drinking in these quiet moments in this special place, gave me a space to calm myself.

On this particular day, as I looked over the stream into the cornfield, on to the other side, it seemed surreal as if I was looking at a different place in time.

Where I stood on my side of the stream, it was bright sunshine and dry, and yet in front of me a heavy rainstorm was in full flow.

The rain formed silver streaks thrashing at the corn which yielded under the weight of the droplets, the stems rustled as if complaining at the interruption of their peace and quiet, then, at that moment the largest brightest rainbow I had ever seen streaked across the sky, the colours were so bright they glowed, as if an artist had just graced the sky with his paint brush,

The corn seemed to stand taller against its forceful intruder, and shone golden, as if in defiance, the breeze then caught hold, and it swayed in a rhythmic dance, bright rays of amber sunlight rose up behind me and danced upon the ears of corn. As a fine spray of rain carried across the stream on the breeze, caressed and bathed my skin.

I felt fresh and new as if I had been baptized into a whole new beginning with a welcoming sense of wellbeing.

It was as if someone had opened a child's picture book to a magical place only found in fairytales. I stood motionless watching the wondrous vision before me, feelings of never wanting this moment to end.

The sun had started to set into the hills behind me, the vibrant colours began to fade as the rays of the sun no longer reached and touched the corn. The rainbow disappeared, and all that remained was a heavy clouded grey sky.

It was as if a light had been suddenly turned off, but not in my heart and mind, the colour's and sight I had witnessed had put a spring in my step, my heart felt so full of joy I thought it would burst.

I headed back up the slope of the fields towards the same gate where only a few weeks before, I had almost ended my life.

The sun was almost out of sight now a fraction of its glowing ember rested on the hill top guiding me home. It seemed to set more quickly than I had remembered, rapidly gloomy shadows formed on the ground in front of me, some darker than others, it seemed like the ground was moving, as I walked the shadows moved away from me with each approaching foot step.

I became aware of dozens of rabbits swiftly scurrying for cover before me. For that short time I had forgotten my pain and unhappiness. 'I was lost in the image of my awakening'

I could hardly contain myself, as I told anyone who would listen about the wonderful event at the stream, only to be greeted with confused and puzzled looks, at my excitement. When I next saw Mary, I told her excitedly about what had happened at the stream.

'Oh yes I have a book about that' she said calmly. She then scanned her eyes across her book shelf, pulling the book from it resting place, and then gave it to me, once again my eager little hands, could not wait to get home and read it.

This was to be my second book to heighten my awareness called
'The Awakener' by Sandy Stevenson.
On the front cover was a picture the same brightness as rainbow I had seen. This book covers a different spiritual angle, based on a planetary vibration and an alien intervention level. At that point in my development, it resonated with me, and yet I didn't understand its significance; it was too advanced for me to comprehend.
It wasn't actually until 2008, I really grasped what they were saying, and how their knowledge and understanding is weaving into present day events. I hadn't understood the enormity and importance of what I was reading and never for a moment thought it could have any bearing on my life, and what I was to do later in life.
In 2011, I began to channel a very different range of energy's. I have no reason not to trust those in the world of spirit, and I carried out the instructions as guided.
11.11.2011 saw an energy grid painted on the floor of my home, with precise instructions, timing.
At the time I wasn't aware that it was in fact the sequel to the work I would be channeling on the 12.12.2012 leading on to the channeling, for the 21.12.2012 transmissions.

From that time on my energy's, and other peoples energy's changed, it was a powerful transmission of specific energy frequencies and vibrations from a higher source of light, that would affect earth and her future, regardless of creed, colour, faiths and beliefs. Had it not occurred then the future would have been very unpleasant for all mankind and mother earth.

We have had and still have reports of unidentified flying Objects (U.F.Os'). Sightings increased before the, transmission governments' saying the public can see their documents that had been secret for many years, and alien TV shows and films on the increase. It has to be said, are the authorities actually getting us used to the idea we are not alone perhaps?

This later work in 2012 was directly linked to the Sandy Stevens book 'The Awakener' at such an early stage in my development it was so important like the Lillian Beck book it went over my head, I wonder how my spiritual life would have evolved if I had have understood them when they were presented to me.

My path at the time in 1998 was a different one and as long as we all work towards the same goal, it does not matter whether you're into planetary peace, enlightenment of mankind or here help to yourself or others, or to help the dead and dying.
We all want the world to be a safer and better place to live.
This will only come about through love, trust, understanding and tolerance of our fellow man.
As for Mother Nature, she has her own laws of survival and these cannot be dominated. It is essential that we all try to live in peace and harmony with her, then we should be better able to help others in times of crisis, and maybe we can save ourselves.

❖

Over the following weeks I would sit by the stream where I had experienced my awakening hoping to see a wondrous sight once more. I felt at peace by the water among the fields and wildlife. One summer evening I sat legs dangling over the sides of the stream's bank as a family of ducks bobbed on by, totally unaware of their observer on the bankside. Pipistrelle bats flew overhead diving down to the waterline, collecting insects; I then discovered that I too was been observed, as a barn owl flew low between the banks of the stream, level with me, his head turned looking directly at me, as our eyes met, the same feeling of exaltation filled me to bursting point.

That freeze fame moment seemed to last for a long time, but in reality it was perhaps only moments. This experience formed a special memory, somewhere deep in my subconscious. I knew this moment was significant for me in some way.

The owl had a meaning for me, I sensed that I was being told something, you will also find that sometimes deep inside you have a sense that an experience is significant, we believe it is a sign or a message, from whatever power you believe in.

When I decided to live on the water it was a cormorant and a flock of Canadian geese that made me realise this is where I should be.

Once again I ran to Mary with my story. She promptly said 'Oh yes, an owl is a symbol of wisdom,' she said, and then loaned me my third book, `My Life as a Medium,' by Betty Shine.

This book became to me like a bible, as it is to Christian. In times of spiritual trouble, Betty Shine's book always provided insight and guidance for me. I could relate her experiences to my own and for the first time in my life I started to know myself; but most importantly of all it, confirmed I wasn't mad.

My life was now changing fast, friends loaned me money; a house came up for rent in the village, called 'HighFields' and on August the eighth 1998, I made my escape with the children. I had very little money and few possessions.

However, as word spread locally, offers of unwanted furniture came flooding in, and within a couple of weeks I had a furnished home and we were well settled in to our new life.

In this house I felt instantly a home, numerous spirits wandering around its small rooms, I never felt afraid, it was so comforting having them there. I felt I was where I belonged and surrounded by those I belonged with.

When I look back I wondered how I had the courage and strength to leave, and to stand alone without support.

Becoming totally independent is a big step for any one.

I had never been without a man before, I assumed that a woman needed a man in order to be whole, or so I had believed. I didn't know a whole new world of independence could bring such adventures and freedom.

This was new and unexpected ground that I was now treading. I had so much wanted the family dream of home, husband and 2.5 children, surrounded by love and happiness.

I came to understand why I had to leave that family dream behind, and now I feel it was all part of a greater plan. I learnt where my courage came from, and why the pattern had to be broke.

A little look at life

Let us take a pause hear and focus on you the reader for a few moments,
Look back yourself, at what life has thrown at you. Look at all those problems you have overcome; a broken heart, abuse, loss of a loved one, a terrible illness, an accident etc.
Remember how you felt at that time, like you could never survive the pain and heartache of the loss. You felt as if your whole world had come to an end. Nevertheless you did survive and you have moved on. You had the strength to overcome life's trials and tribulations and you came out the other side. Maybe a bit battered and worse for wear, no matter how hard it was.
Take a moment to give yourself the praise you deserve, a pat on your own back, life is not easy. However, we all learn valuable lessons from these life experiences and these are the building blocks for our survival. So well done you!

Life is life and it bites us in the bum, when we least expect it, the spiritual side is there to draw on and I can assure you it will help you through.
The more connected you are the more easily you find the strength to overcome your difficulties. So hang in there friend, you can cope with all challenges with help from spirit.
Let go of anger, regret, shame, heartache, jealousy etc.
As these negative things hold you back, as they build up within you and cause you more problems.
An example which I was given to use, was as follows.
I felt a great deal of anger towards my husband at the time, which lasted long after I left him. It chewed and ate at my

insides, the anger that I didn't let out built up, until it felt like physical pain.

Around this time I had been loaned a selection of tapes by Mary, one day as I listened and worked with a tape by Louise Hay, I followed the instructions.

I was told to take that person you were angry with and imagine them shrinking back into a small child, and then take them into my heart. This was hard very hard to do, taking someone who had hurt you so badly, and making them into a small child. I did as instructed be it, with difficulty and gritted teeth. When I got up the next morning I felt lighter and newer in some way; all my anger had melted away like a snowflake on a warm window.

The Message

Now in the safety of 'HighFields' my new home, with wall to wall spirits to keep me company, material things appeared like magic. I felt at peace and contented; I had begun to study massage. I juggled between working in a public house and cleaning other houses, money wasn't too much of an issue, and although little money was left over after the bills, I always seemed to make ends meet.

Little did I know that yet to come, there was confusion and arguments between logic and the psychic, which would disturb my peace and contentment.

Those small seeds planted back in 1974 at Jetta house, I then did not question the spiritual and psychic activity's, trusting as a child trusts, now as an adult I had lost the innocent trusting of a child, and adult mind was in the driving seat.

The peace and calm unfortunately was not to last,

It became clear that I had in fact a job to do for the world of spirit seeing them and hearing them was part of the normal day's events, nevertheless working for them had not entered my head, the only knowledge I had to date was, what I had read of Betty shines, and Sandy Stevens.

It wasn't known to me at the time but spirit had already lined me up for my first spiritual task back in 1996 when I was still at the farm.

I had a series of dreams and these dreams were to shape my future having a flowing effect all the way through my life to the very point I am now.

It became clear that those dreams were in fact a message I had to deliver from the world of spirit to a man who would give me a key to another door. However at the time I did not know this. And the simple task of delivering a message was enough to send me into total panic and confusion which was self-inflicted.

❖

Now ask yourself how difficult can it be to give someone a
message? You just walk up them and pass the message on,
right, easy enough wouldn't you say, well not quite that easy.
The message I had to give had been given to me a year before I
had left the farm, and it was another year before I even met the
person, I had to deliver the message to, It wasn't a verbal
message like, `Ask him to get me three pints of milk, and a loaf
of bread.'
This message started for me as a series of dreams, played over
and over for a number of weeks, like a video tape, until every
detail was fixed firmly in my mind, so firmly I can still recall
each one as vividly as I could eighteen years ago when they
first came to me.
These dreams felt completely real, I could smell, feel, hear and
see everything as if I was experiencing the events in the flesh.

The First Dream

This dream saw me on a lonely country road at night, driving
my dad's old Volkswagen caddy-truck.
I drove along the rain soaked road, flooded by the full light of
the new moon; it shone as bright as a sun suspended in a clear
star spangled sky. I drove along following the twists and turns
of the road, as it snaked through the open fields, there were no
hedgerows, animals, or trees, just clear open space. I felt calm
and peaceful, my thoughts then made me aware of the truck
stopping, and the vehicle came to a halt. I climbed out of the
truck and started to walk, even though I did not know the place
I was in, I seemed to know where I was going. I walked across
the wet grass feeling my feet sink a little into the wet ground
with each step. Ahead of me I could see the shape of an old
limestone building, reaching up in the moonlit sky with tall

chimneys silhouetted in its luminosity. My calm feeling began to dissolve giving way to fear. In that instance a sense of panic took over me. I turned to run in the opposite direction back to my truck.

As I turned on my heels I became aware of a large number of men and women stood behind me in the distance.

The sky is aglow with fire; they had set my truck alight.

I start to panic, my heart pounds in my chest and my throat is so dry, it hurts. I know, I have no option but to go to the stone building for protection, although it is the last thing I want to do. The people walk towards me with staring unblinking eyes and expressionless faces. No words are spoken, they are wrapped in winter clothing, and the night sky is still aglow behind them. I turn and walk faster to the building, I have no means of escape, I have no choice, my footsteps quicken along with the pounding of my heart, I turn once more to look back, they are closing in on me and following me still. I can see the walls of the house, old stone with moss growing over the walls. I know inside a man dressed in black waits for me, I really don't want to go in.......!

The Second Dream,

I find myself on the outskirts of a small town, ahead is a market on a grassy hillside, with French style cafes, scattered in the square below. I wander round the stalls, which are selling strange and unusual objects. Many of which I don't recognize. I am followed by a man in beige robes with a long white beard, he doesn't speak to me, and he just walks close behind me.

The man in black sits at a table outside one of the café's in the square. I sense I have to go to him. However I take too long as I'm intrigued and happy to explore theses strange surrounding. By the time I turn to go down the hillside to where he was siting he has left. I feel an overwhelming feeling of sadness,

with a choked up sensation in my throat, that I have in fact
missed him....

Third Dream

It is a warm summer day and I am once more in the
countryside, walking up a long winding road, to a house that
sits at the top of the hill. I walk up the hill, with ease feeling
calm and relaxed. When I reach the house, I enter through a
wooden gate that is in need of repair and a coat of paint.
The cottage's garden looks a little unkempt.
I am facing the gable-end of the house, in which is set a white
painted front door, I open the door and walk in; I entered and
sensed he is expecting me. A highly polished old wooden floor
lies before me; it has wider width floorboards than a normal
floor. There is a hat stand to the left as I walk in. I hear clearly
the smooth and even tick-tock of some old clock resounding
through the entrance hall with a steady soothing rhythm.
The air is filled with an aroma of an era gone by, it is that
unmistakable smell that tells you this is a house that has stood
for many years, and seen so many things.
The smells filter through my nostrils, giving me that feeling of
connection I had experienced as a child. I turn to look to my
right, the first half of a staggered wooden staircase faces me,
and the second half turns sharply to the left. The whole
structure is edged by a thick wooden bannister, at the top of the
first flight of stairs, there's a large un-curtained arch shaped
window, the sunlight floods though illuminating every nook
and cranny of this majestic old house, the polished wood floor
gleaming in its rays, the grain and colour of the old timber
floor boards highlighted, in vibrant rich browns and gold's;
energetic and full of life. I see the man in black walking down
the stairs to greet me, as he reaches the last step, I go to meet

him, he is taller than I am and when I look up I can't see his face, only light.......!

The Fourth Dream

This time I was in a collage complex of some sort, it was warm and seemed like a continental environment and the area was covered in a red type of soil. The evening sun burnished the whole place in an autumn gold light.

I and the man in black are stood on the balcony looking down on a courtyard, surrounded by so much peace and calm, that rests within the peoples' hearts below. Lovers hold hands, smile and gaze at each other, people are content and happy. However, all is not as it seems, I am tugging at the man in blacks arm, saying, 'We must get the people out.'

I say this with a sense of urgency in my voice; I repeat this over and over. I feel his heartfelt pain, as if it is my own and his loss, of a dream. The feelings are that the foundations are unsafe.......

The dreams repeated themselves over and over in my head, until they were firmly locked in my mind, I slotted them away in my subconscious with all the other spiritual and psychic events, that were taking place at the farm In my unhappy situation I hoped it was the handsome prince that would one day come and rescue me.

It was about a year after the dreams started that I had met Mary, and as you will recall from the earlier chapter, she became my friend, guide and Reiki Master.

One day she came to visit me as usual, just before I left the farm.

'Here,' she said, handing me a cassette tape, with the back of the box facing me 'Music for the Heart' she said in a casual matter of fact way.

I took the tape from her and turned it over so that I could see the front cover; I could hardly believe my eyes,

'It's him,' I blurted out, 'It's the man in the dreams.'

On the front cover of the tape was a picture of a man in the dreams wearing the same suit, and looking exactly as I seen him.

'Perhaps you're going to give him a message,' Mary said in passing with no real excitement.

I didn't pay much attention to what she had said, I didn't know about medium-ship and messages, how I wished I had asked Mary, 'What do you mean message?' If I had done so at that time, I may have saved myself such a lot of torment, or would I? And the name of the tape!

'Heartland'

I had been attuned to Reiki the June of 1998 just before I left the farm, two weeks after the reiki attunment the things I needed to make my escape appeared like magic, and less than two months later on august the eighth I was in the safety of Highfields.

Following doing my Reiki One the shadows before someone's death disappeared, as Mary had said they would, and my vibrations became higher.

My psychic development had taken a vast leap forwards, and my third eye was more active and I began to grow.

The abilities that I had been born with that had almost withered and died were now being nurtured and nourished, I was growing fast in my new plant- pot, my chakra energy centers started to clear, my mind and body began to heal.

The house HighFields was my sanctuary, peace and calm rained down on me and mine, I felt a last that I could breath, I felt like a bird that had been locked up in a cage for a very long time; now the cage door wasn't just open but broken off its hinges, I was free to fly. I felt whole and strong.

Then I made a promise, to never to let myself be caged again. This new found peace and calm at HighFields I soon discovered was not to last long, with wall to wall spirits coming for a quick look, at this odd mortal that was well aware of the unseen world that she now shared.

My abilities to sense energies had sharpened; I was beginning to absorb other people's energies like a sponge in water. Spirit attachments jumped in and out of my aura as they pleased, and I was better run than a Leeds number sixty five bus. I was surrounded by voices, messages, signs, sightings just to name a few of the spiritual events that down loaded into my life.

On top of this a new problem, as logic and psyche started battling it out for supremacy. I questioned everything I saw and heard over and over again, not only did I question my sanity but asked

'Why was I like this?'

'What am I supposed to do with it?'

'Am I really seeing and hearing all this?'

'What the hell am I?'

'Where are the others like me?'

'Am I insane, do I need to phone the men in the white van? Who would coax me into going quietly with them for half a pound of jelly babies'

Then there was all the excitement at each new psychic hurdle crossed and the childlike exhilaration,

'That's amazing, really cool, do it again….. Aw please'

Then in popped the logic, doing a good job of trying to convince me I was crazy, the adult logical mind,

'Don't be stupid it's not real, it's all in your imagination or fantasy.'

At this time Mary and my path began to travel in different directions, she had begun her new path of personal growth, and I missed her so much. We saw little of each other, and this is where, I began to have the familiar feelings of being isolated, and alone. Even though I was surrounded by family and friends, I didn't speak of my spiritual battles and events for fear of being judged as insane. No one around me knew I was on a spiritual path, and that I had in fact more dead people as friends than living. I was back to the familiar and unhappy feeling of being the odd one out, not feeling I belonged any were, and very alone. Even with the world of spirit by my side.

By this time I had trained in massage, aromatherapy, and practice on neighbours and friends. And while giving the treatment spirit would relay messages to me in picture form, I had come to the conclusion that the world of spirit used the treatments as the carrot to entice the donkey; it was just a way of getting them through the door, so the universal light could do its work. I worked with many people and I often knew some of the physical and mental pain they suffered. Sometimes they would confirm the thoughts I was sensing as delivered the therapy, and others would hide or avoid what was going on, my instincts kept me well informed of what I could say and to whom. The clients didn't know I was in communication with spirit they just assumed it was part of the reiki which in a way it was. My real secret remained well guarded

I was feeling very lonely and yearned for people who would understand me and my hidden life. I had many spirits to guide and help me. However, I still wanted so much to meet a mortal guide to help me through, a guru or some kind of spiritual teacher.

I wanted to grow and put my abilities to good use, not for myself but for others.

I soon came to realise that my training was to be an isolated affair, until 2002; a brief interlude and then alone again till 2005 and then until 2010 when the reason behind the dreams, and going to the man in black in person came to the fore.

I was becoming more accepting and accustomed to the real me and I loved and trusted the world of spirit without question. Until... logic prodded me, reminding me this was not normal, I must be imagining everything, and that I was in fact quite deranged.

I would then feel safe in the knowledge that spirit were guiding me and protecting me. Then in would jump logic 'It's all in your head, your delusional'

Then feelings of comfort knowing spirit were there with me even when things were not going well, or I did not understand, I would ask why was this or that happening?

Although I knew I would get through it, and its outcome would turn out for my highest good, even though at times I could not see it, not just throwing teddy out of the pram, resorting to pulling his ears off and jumping all over him too.

Among the changes within me, the message I had had at the farm, which I had received in the four dreams; were taking shape and becoming clearer as time passed.

I had bought a copy of the 'Heartland' tape Mary had introduced me to.

I didn't understand why at the time, it started to affect me deeply with it sounds and vibrations. I did not know at this time in my development how sound vibrations can heal.

It just felt as if the music was soaking into my very heart and soul. I didn't understand how I could be so moved.

`Heartland`, is still the main album of music I draw on when I need strength or feel alone and need a deeper connection to the realms, that lay beyond the world of spiritual practices, it brings a feeling like that of going home.

The reason for the dreams were becoming clear, and in spirits, magical way, a brochure appeared through my letterbox for the `Mind, Body and Spirit Festival' in Manchester, a picture of the` Heartland' tape's musician was on the front cover, if only I had taken note of Mary's words,
'Maybe you are going to give him a message' she had said
Needless to say her words had fallen on deaf ears earlier.
So I began to piece my jigsaw together, with my Sherlock Homes head on.
I knew the dreams were for the man on the tape cover.
They were a message he would understand.
I knew his name, what he looked like and where he was going to be on a certain date. 'It's elementary my dear Watson'
Then the Logic and psyche started their arguments yet again, with a good helping of self-doubt and disbelief playing a part too. I said to myself, 'Why me?
Why not someone else who was closer to him and who knew him better, would that not be more appropriate?
I'm not sure how I will I get there? I didn't even know what the dreams were about. I had never met him or heard of him till the tape…
Then I had a flash of logic, 'don't be silly it's all imagination, coincidence….forget it. '
Spirit continued with my training constantly backing up what they were showing and saying to me. However me being me, I would then create an obstacle, each time they gave me evidence regarding a specific message they gave me.

Spirit would then again show me more evidence, giving
logic the boot, if only temporally.
As the next part story will show, sometimes they scared me for
my own good to get their message across.

I sat one evening watching television at HighFields, when the
women in the play on television screamed,
'Manchester, Manchester, we love you,' she shouted it several
times; the words began ringing in my ears not to be dismissed
lightly. I knew the festival was at Manchester, while analyzing
this light bulb moment, a spirit of a young man appeared in my
kitchen doorway, and he was a surprised to see me as I was
him. I didn't have time to think it all happened so fast, he
turned and he walked off through the wall of the bathroom.
I must admit his solid appearance nearly caused a change of
underwear for me. I looked at the television once again and
still the actress was shouting,
'Manchester I love you.'
Feeling a bit shell shocked, I plucked up the courage to go to
the kitchen, logic saying there was someone in the house, and
the psychic knowing the man I saw was a spirit.
The day before this event I had been on the bus to town and I
saw an ambulance parked by the river Trent; I didn't know it at
the time but a young man had drowned and they were there
recovering his body. When I saw him that night, he seemed to
be running and had passed through HighFields, on his journey
to be wherever he was going

I filtered through my fuddled brain, what I had seen that
evening and I knew spirit were making it quite clear they

wanted me to go to Manchester. I found also they were even projecting images to my brother who knew nothing of what I was involved in.

A few days after the spirit event, my brother came to stay with me, as he lay on the treatment couch I gave him Reiki, he recounted that whilst I had been treating him, he had seen a man in black. The man had been walking in an ancient grave yard, with large yew trees at the entrance. I had in also seen the image in my mind too. In my version the man in black was resting his hand on ancient stones the remnants of a gate way. The grass on the land was in stiff wind swept tussocks, scorched brown by wind and sun.

I didn't say to my brother, I knew who the man was.

The thoughts of should I or shouldn't I go to Manchester, were constantly filling my head, I was in total confusion, logic saying it was imagination, spirit making it quite clear it was not.

Spirit was determined that I was going to give this message to him, no matter how many excuses I made, and I was exceptionally good at those. One excuse was how would I get there? I couldn't drive there; I was a chicken when it came to driving in towns, especially big ones I don't know. Once again due to their instance that I would follow my task

It was a summer evening warm and bright, about seven o'clock and I went to Kelham Hall to collect my electoral role documents, at that time I worked for The Register of Electors, and well as a public house and cleaning, and it was normal practice to go to the council offices in the evening to collect our boxes of paper work.

I parked the car and then started to walk across the car park there wasn't anyone around apart from two women stood in the car park talking. As I passed them I heard one say,

'Did you drive to Manchester then?'

The other replied, 'No I caught the train.'
I was well aware that this was a spiritual signpost, I had to go
to Manchester to deliver the message and now they had told me
how. Once again logic jumped in
'It's just coincidence…..why me? I don't even know
him…..what am i going to say to a total stranger?
As the festival date approached, I spent most of my waking
moments worrying and fretting about giving the message, spirit
was quite insistent and another signpost was given to me.

As I waited to cross the road I turned to secure my sons hand,
and I just glimpsed over my shoulder in to the library window
nearby, there in the window stood one solitary book, with the
title 'A to Z of Manchester.' My name is Angela Zillah,
'Ok I'll go' I said out loud.
However peace did not come with my agreeing to go, negative
spirits popped in and out, now aware I was going to do as
asked by Light Spirits', they used my self-worth, and
confidence concepts and beliefs to try to stop me, negative
spirits taking sides with logic to gain an advantage.
When I was in a doubtful mood, saying all the things that were
happening were imaginary, my instability shouted out
inwardly,
'Give it all up wouldn't life be so much easier' they repeated
over and over again.
And of course logic and my psychic side battled for supremacy
right up until I actually did the deliver the message.
Remember the book 'Into the light' by Lillian Beck, recalling
the passage about
'People are rarely able to handle it and become unstable.'

In amongst all this interaction was the normal spiritual growth
and the added fact I was very lonely. I had no one to ask about
the events and I yearned so, for a mortal spiritual companion.

I had begun the electoral role work around the same time when the inner battle was in full flow which I told you about above. I was at the time carrying out the required door to door knocking to collect electoral role information from householder. As I did this work I found as the people opened their doors, I sensed what they were feeling, so many emotions from hundreds of houses, which I soaked up like a sponge. It made me feel depressed, anxious, confused, sick, angry and afraid. I didn't want to feel other people's emotions. Where were the nice emotions like joy and happiness; It seemed that they were few and far between, but they must have been there somewhere, Why was I was only picking up on negative emotions.

I realised quite some time later that the people I was filling the forms out with were dumping their personal rubbish energies onto me, and in some way.

I needed to earth them or pass them through without harming myself or anyone else. I knew I needed some sort of protection, but what?

So I began to search for a solution, all I had to support me in the physical world at this time was the `Kindred Spirit' magazine, which gave me the comforting notion that I wasn't alone that there were others out there like me.

I had seen an advert sometime earlier, in the magazine, for a metal disk called a selfic, they claimed would help to protect you, when working with spirit. When I looked for the advert, I was skeptical, I scanned through the magazine. On finding the advert I filled out the form and sent away for the selfic disk. The seller asked for my date of birth and name, as it was to be programmed specifically for me and no one else could ever use it, I didn't know at that point in my growth about sacred geometry and vibrations. And those items could be programed with these.

It was made by Damanhur in Italy and they also made a range of 'Selfic' jewelry to assist people with a range of problems. They have a web-site and books that are in my opinion well worth reading.

So a few days later the Selfic disk arrived, not being someone who believed in talisman, or so I thought, I was unconvinced at the claims, and wondered why I had spent seventeen pounds on an ornate bit of metal. As I had really didn't have money to splash around things were getting very tight financially.

I placed it down on the side feeling a little cross with myself. My daughter who was fourteen at the time came in to my room,

'What's this ..? She said picking it up, only to put it down in double quick time, 'I can feel its energy,' she showed signs of not liking the sensation, that event in itself was unusual as I said very little about my new age world to the children.

She promptly wandered away as quickly as she had appeared. I wondered how she knew it was energy, she could feel.

I picked the disk up, and I felt nothing at all.

'Well I may as well try it' I said to myself and put it on a piece of cord around my neck.

That night I went to bed still wearing the Selfic disk, I lay looking into the darkness that enveloped the room; sleep had not yet come over me. I weighed up my days events and what was on the list for the following day, not even thinking about the selfic disk.'

As I lay in my bed globules of colours unexpectedly appeared about an arms-length away from me. I dismissed them as patterns caused by the lamplight; I had turned it off a few minutes earlier, I lay there waiting for them to disappear as they should have.

The colours then moved towards me becoming larger as they moved nearer and nearer, I blinked my eyes a few times expecting them to stop, they didn't.

I sat up in bed, 'It can't be real' my logic mind said.
I wasn't sure what was happening, 'It must be my eyes playing tricks' I thought dismissing them once more, the globules began to change colour, they became red on the outside with black centres, they turned and undulated around, moving about as if they were being pulled one direction then a another direction, and then they would split into two half's like an amoeba dividing its self.
The colours then changed to orange with a turquoise center, rotating then moving before changing yet again, they split in two, this time they became yellow and green.
I kept blinking my eyes it wasn't the light bulb that had caused this and I was sat up in bed 'Yes I was wide awake'
I could see my room in the evening darkness the shapes of furniture, the light form outside through the curtains this was real, and it was not the result of a light bulb.
The yellow and green globules moved as before and this time they changed into triangular shapes of pale green with pink mottled centers, they were constantly moving and shifting, moving in one direction and then another, twisting turning but always joined, It was like I was inside a kaleidoscope, and now logic faded and left me to enjoy the spectacle. I watched fascinated, like a small child never wanting this show to end.
It then found myself in totally darkness as if all light had be extinguished form the room, I saw the silhouette of myself, in the universe, I stood before a full sized planet, that as traveling at a steady pace towards me, I just stood still and it passed through me as if I was a ghost. I turn my head to follow its direction as it went behind me. But the image had vanished.
I turned back looking to the foot of my bed still awake still sat up, hardly able to believe what I had just seen, I was lost in the total wonder of the experience, when two translucent blue, slightly built delicate figures appeared with movements like flickering flames. The energies of the room changed and for

the first time I now began to feel a little unnerved. As I watched them, part of me wanted to ask questions and the other part of me didn't know what to say, they flickered and waivered, then a new awareness overcame me, of two large dark blocks, like pillars of energy rose up either side of me. For the first time since the phenomenon started I was afraid. I said out loud, 'If you come in the name of light you are welcome if not go away' my voice was spluttering out the words, I was too scared to look, giving only brief side wards glance.

My fear did not last long and it melted away as a reassuring calmness seeped over me, something else was forming and I became lost in another revelation, as a large golden labyrinth appeared before me, vibrant oranges and reds merged and mingled as if it was molten rock or metal and so vividly bright. I could see the shape of the spiral and the sides of the walls, becoming larger as I felt myself start moving forward towards the labyrinth, as if I was sat in the driving seat of a car, I begin to pick up speed, faster and faster into the labyrinth I went twisting and turning this way and that avoiding a collision, with the sides further and further into its golden spirals. Although it was fast, I felt safe, with whatever was happening to me, it was an amazing feeling.

Then it just stopped, no warning no gentle slowing down, it just stopped, and everything disappeared as quickly as it had appeared. I so didn't want it to stop. I sat in the darkness looking around, but there was nothing. No colours, planet, blue flames, nothing left at all.

I was exhilarated by the experience and also disappointed that it had stopped. I flopped back onto my pillows wondering what I had just experienced; I was most certainly wide awake.

I tried many times sitting in the darkness with the Selfic disk, hoping that something as wonderful once more would appear, to this day it has never happened again.

From that day onwards I treat the selfic disk with love and respect, over the years it is as if it is a person and has its own way of letting me know when I must wear it and when not to, It is like a telepathic communication, not unlike the world of spirit. It has given me protection from those in this world and the next, in the early days it aided communication with spirit, and I know now that it in fact grows and adjusts with me, and my abilities it feels as if it is a living entity
It's the best seventeen pounds I ever spent!
I wore my Selfic disk a lot of the time, in my earlier days of growth and transformation.
It did not help with the battle within me though; my logical and psychic self were still trying to better one another all the time day after day. These were lessons of a different kind.
And my lack of confidence in myself was a big factor.
Despite the friction between logic and psychic, I was aware of the task I had to do for the world of spirit to deliver the message to the man in black.
Eighteen years to date at the time of final editing; I understand why they chose me to deliver the message and yet I don't know what the final outcome will be.

So at this point of my growth the year is late 1999, I had logic and the psychic arguing, with each other, negative spirits trying to do their best to stop me continuing working for the world of spirit, natural growth and development, soaking up energies of others like a sponge, working bring up a family, running a home, and more dead friends than live ones, and the only thing to remind me that I wasn't insane was the kindred spirit magazine.
I knew I had to deliver the message about the dreams, and who the message was for. I knew where, when and how to get there, and at this time, I still didn't know why I was chosen for the task.

Three weeks before the 'Mind Body and Spirit Festival' in
Manchester, my weight dropped by a stone in two weeks I
wasn't hungry, I didn't feel weak or ill in any way, in fact I felt
good physically, even though the inner battle continued.
Spirit continued to give me clear signs and messages, to keep
my mind on the task ahead, throwing in a signpost along the
way at every opportunity.
Even at one point stopping the Heartland tape as it played. As
I turned to see why it had stopped playing, it started again but
the voice did not sing it talked clearly, it said 'The time has
come, the time is now'
Several times, I rewound the tape to see if it would speak again
and to this day it never has.
In my daily conversations with spirit I grumbled at them,
complaining about how difficult my task was, 'It is so
complicated' I moaned.
'Only as complicated as you make it' came the sharp reply.
Now I had accepted the task, my next question was,
 'How, was I going to give this message to a total stranger?'
Confidence was not my strong point, and the answer came with
my newly acquired computer, and I admit I wasn't quite sure
what I was doing with it. I actually became somewhat excited
when I could switch it on, it lit up, and I could write on the
white screen, be It one finger at a time and very, very slowly.
So the words flowed and the letter for the man in black was
written. When I read it back to myself I was well aware that I
had help in writing it, it was from the heart, and the wording
was not mine.
I booked tickets for the G Mex Centre in Manchester, for the
mind body and spirit festival, where I knew the man in black
would be, I had arranged train tickets for my friend Sue and I;
We set off on our journey, as we travelled I told my friend
everything that had happened, I just blabbed it all out,

I told her about the message that the spirit world had asked me to deliver, and the sign posts. Sue didn't look the least bit surprised or shocked; she didn't doubt a word of what I had said, or even comment. It was as if it was a normal daily common occurrence I later discovered she had in fact a very natural gifted tarot reader.

We eventually reached the G Mex Centre. I was very nervous, and once inside the energies gained the upper hand. I couldn't think clearly, my head became so muddled I was in a total daze. I put my Selfic disk on in order to keep the negative energies out; within ten minutes I was fine. I had located the man in black's stand; where he was based and from where he was hosting the stage events.

His stand was near the stage and a noticed a lady stood with him. My nerves started to build up again my heart pounded in my chest; my throat was very dry, just like in the dreams. I was about to deliver a message that had been given to me some two years ago there was no turning back.

Several times I approach his stand, and several times I walked away, as my courage left me once more; eventually I took the easy option and waited until the lady who was with him was alone. I walked over to her, and I told her about the message, she was very kind and supportive and said, 'You must tell him. He would want to know, he will be back in a minute' she said looking around to see if she could see him. I left the stand after making the excuse that I would call back later. I walked away and began to look around the other stands at the festival.

Even though my development was in its infancy, I felt different and although only thirty nine years old, I felt older.

I sensed so many people with outreaching hands, reaching out desperately looking for something to hold on to. They were desperate for guidance, healing, messages from lost loved ones, posing questions, what will the future hold?

So many reaching! For what?

I knew many of them only had to look inside themselves to find what they were seeking.

Often you will find people don't look inside themselves first, it is too simple a solution, and so much more difficult, for them to trust their inner thoughts and feelings.

Eventually I plucked up courage and approached the man in black's stand at a quiet moment during the day. I opened my mouth to relay his message, the one that had caused me so many sleepless nights, so many arguments between psychic and the logic mind.

Nothing came out, like a fish gasping for air, my words were non-existent, I held out the letter I had previously written with the wonders of my new computer, the envelope looking somewhat crumpled after the vice like nervous grip I had held on to it throughout the day.

He took it from me, 'I should read this,' he asked?

I responded like a nodding donkey from an oil field.

He showed no surprise as if it was nothing out of the ordinary, as I now know it is, he thanked me warmly, saying

'He would read it' placing it in his top pocket on his jacket and patting it reassuringly.

I shuffled away feeling quite stupid.

However the task was completed and I had done as spirit had asked. It was over, done with, finished, I felt instant relief; I had completed my task be it with some large hiccups and forceful persuasion.

As usual spirit had other ideas unbeknown to me they were not done with me yet.

As my friend and I watched the show, a spirit voice told me to give the man in black my crucifix, I was reluctant to do so, I had, had it for so long I couldn't remember where it came from, and with a verbal ear battering from my spiritual teachers, I took the silver cross and chain from around my neck taking one last look at the small silver flowers engraved upon it.

As he left the stage I placed it in his hand with jumbled words of, 'They asked me to do things, I didn't know why' he thanked me kindly.

Again I felt so stupid but at least I didn't argue with spirit, and logic remained very quiet.

Later that evening I saw my friend Sue safely on to the train back home to Newark. I had decided to book myself into a hotel for the night previously thinking we would perhaps both be staying, intending to spend the next day again at the festival at the G Mex.

I set off from the station, and caught the tram back to the G mex, I knew exactly where to go, a short walk from the tram stop to my hotel, a nice dinner and a long soak in a bubble bath before a good night's sleep, my work for spirit was done and I planned the next day to simply enjoy the G mex show and stalls and treat myself to something nice.

I had seen the hotel roof sign from a higher level while in the G mex and I could see the front entrance of the hotel from the pedestrian crossing as I began to cross the road from the G Mex Centre. I had no reason not to feel confident I knew where I was going, Or so I thought, It didn't take me long to find myself lost in the dark rainy streets of Manchester.

I wandered around for quite some time, I could see the roof top sign of the hotel high above the streets; no matter which way I walked I just couldn't seem to reach it. I walked around and around, asking how to reach it from passersby and even the directions from others didn't seem to help me at all.

I was getting cold, tired and hungry and starting to feel sorry for myself.

I eventually found the entrance to the hotel across the road from the G Mex, I questioned myself yet again. How I could have possibly got lost in the first place. It was just where I had crossed the road earlier, I realised that I needed to earth the day's energies, and getting lost in the darkness and rain certainly did that.

Feeling very hungry, I was looking forward to the luxury of a comfortable hotel room and nice meal in the restaurant.

I ordered fish with neapolitan sauce and herb salad.

The meal, was nothing like the menu stated the sauce was in fact a cold salsa, only fitting to grace a packet of pringles crisps, and no herb salad, in fact no salad at all, I asked the waitress for the salad and was well aware that the chef was not impressed, the waitress presented me with a very, very, large bowl of rocket lettuce leaf. Having been in the catering trade for many years, I was well aware I had upset the chef, I'm not one to complain, however I did ask the waitress to thank the chef and point out I wasn't a rabbit.

My instincts told me not to eat it.

I went to my room, I was weary and it had been quite a day, I welcomed the thought of a good night's sleep, after a nice bubble bath, then a nice breakfast in the morning. I felt pleased, that the day was over.

All the messages, signs, dreams, and spirits insistence, was done and dusted along with an added feeling of being quite foolish at my lack of confidence, I had done as they asked and now I was free.

The hotel was a tower block type structure; and my room was situated at the back of the hotel, situated on a corner, its windows spanned the whole length of the main wall, overlooking the canal below. It was the number five hundred and fifty three or there a bouts, I can't recall the exact number now, I do remember it was very high up; looking down on the darkened streets of Manchester and the dark eerie waters of the canal snaking through the buildings, the odd glimmer of street lights casting brief undulating silhouettes within its dark depth's.

I prepared myself for a night of well needed sleep laying down on the bed, I drifted away under willing heavy eyelids with thoughts of tomorrow it would be a more relaxed day, and I thought about the things I would do, I had seen a man from the at the Arthurian stand in the café and I knew I need to talk to him, but didn't know why, interesting the Arthurian stand followed the same theme of belief as the Sandy Stevens Awakener book, my plan was to just enjoy the second day.

I slept for no more than an hour, when I was suddenly awoken, by nothing that I could remember, other than my feet hit the ground and I was stood up wide awake and stood facing the wall.

My heartbeat had risen, my eyes were wide open, like a startled rabbit in headlights, this had never happened to me before, I just stood there not quite sure whether I was in fact asleep and dreaming, as I became more coherent and conscious I realised that I was wide awake.

I turned around to look around the room, and became aware, I was not alone, as a fragrance of flowers filled the air around me. Spirit were making me aware of their presence; the energies of the room began to change, the air became stifling and heavy I felt like I could not breath, my logic kicked in telling me this could not happen, the air-conditioning was on, I could hear it.

I could then see changes in the patterns on the furnishings, changing colours, but not anything, as pleasant as the visions with the selfic disk, this felt unnatural as faces started to appear in the fabric of the curtains, at the same time, as the room took on a surreal feeling, I felt like I was in some sort of dream, and yet I knew I was wide awake.

The energies were becoming far too heavy for me to cope with, I didn't like what I was sensing or feeling, I didn't feel safe or loved, something was wrong, something did not add up. My heart was pounding and the dry feeling in my throat as the adrenalin kicked in fight or flight. To run was my first thought, but it was late and dark outside and I was alone, no were to run, no one to turn to, and too afraid to face what was going on or even understand what was happening in the room. Panic set in, a strong smell of incense now filled the air, to the point I felt I would suffocate, I just couldn't catch my breath. I moved over to the window and slid myself onto the windowsill sitting side ways, tucking my knees up under my chin fixing my gaze out over the streets of Manchester, watching the cities night time activities, trying not to be aware of what was taking place around me,

Voices whispered in the soft lighting, breezes of energies forms made themselves known, touching me, whispering against my ears, trying to gain my attention; my eyes were fixed, on the streets below, those dark soulless looking waters of the canal. My grip on my knees firm I was staying put. I was having none of this. I was so afraid, I had no one to call, no one to ask for help, I thought of the man in black he would know what to do. I didn't know where he was, I didn't have any phone numbers of any one who could help me.

I froze, and kept my gaze rigid on the scenes below me, the streets seemed quite deserted for a Saturday night, for a busy city, there should be hustle and bustle; emptying night clubs and crowds, the streets seemed deserted, I looked through the spaces in the buildings, were the streets were well lit, there was a lack of vehicles it felt like I was the only person alive. Everything felt wrong and out of place.

I could see the murky canal waters below me and the lights as they cast there sinister shadows in the motionless gloomy waters, this only added to the feeling that I wasn't there in a hotel room in Manchester. It was like something from science fiction movie nothing made sense.

All this made my situation seem even more dream like. Yet here I was waiting for the sun to bring the dawn to my rescue, like in a horror movie where the heroine is waiting to see if she survives the night, from the horrors that lurk in the nightfall. I wasn't sure what was taking place at that time, I didn't understand, all I knew is that I felt too afraid to look around me. I had an overwhelming feeling of being very isolated and uncomfortable, at that moment if I had have had somewhere to run or someone to run to, I would have made all haste to reach them; and you wouldn't have seen my heals for dust. However I had nothing and no one to turn to once more I felt totally isolation in this unseen world which merged with mine. My only option was to stay where I was, and so I sat all night on the window sill clutching my knees as close to my chest as tight as I possibly could. Watching waiting, praying for the night to end soon, I can't even remember whether the night seemed long or short. All I remember was waiting, and being too afraid to look into my room.

When the dawn eventually started to break over this sleeping city, I felt like I had survived something terrible and yet I didn't know what. It was so comforting to see the night sky changing from indigo, to violet and eventually lightening to a turquoise blue. The energies of the room had also begun to change, dawn signaling to these entities it was time for them to retreat from where ever they had come from.

Although I sensed the changes in the energies, I stayed on the window sill still too afraid to move clutching my knees witnessing Manchester wakening from its slumber.

As the first rays of the cool morning sun hit the window a wave of relief filled every bone in my body, my tense muscles relaxed and the morning energies felt quite different to that of the night time. I had survived whatever had taken place, even if it was in a cowardly way.

The morning sun light filtered through the room and it looked so different in the day light, pretty yellow curtains, pastel shade colored walls, tasteful pictures, wide white window sills, and a bright neat airy room, there was nothing to fear now. Nevertheless the adrenalin was still pumping, and the fight or flight syndrome flooding my mind and I promptly headed for the shower.

I packed quickly and was ready to leave long before the streets of Manchester came alive, it was six o'clock in the morning, and I waited counting the minutes to freedom perched on the edge of the bed like a greyhound in a trap. Waiting and clock watching, for the time I could, head out, catch my train, and run back to the safety of home.

My beloved Highfields were, the wall to wall spirits would hold me in the loving light.

As soon as the hands clicked eight o'clock, it was time; I left the hotel like a scolded cat, missing breakfast. I had only one thing on my mind home!

The rays of bright sunlight hit me with full force, along with the cool morning air, as it washed over my body, reaffirming the night was over and I was liberated, and free, I pushed the glass doors of the hotel open to freedom!

I could see the Metro Line in the distance to my left across the road, and made my way to the nearest crossing point and then headed for the entrance to the Metro Line, I had ridden it the night before taking Sue to her train, a spirit voice saying quite clearly in my ear telling me 'Go back to the G Mex Centre' I refused point blank with a defiant 'No I have done what you asked, I have had no sleep, I'm grumpy, hungry and I'm going home now' I said. I was adamant I was going home; it had been my original plan to stay the Sunday too. After the events of the night before, there was only one direction I was going and nothing was going to stop me.

The urge to get away from Manchester was strong and I strode out in the direction of the Metro, I could feel negative energies battering my already tiered, fuddled, mind and body. 'Run, run away, go home' a voice whispered, and I was more than willing to oblige.

I had been walking for some time and I seemed to be going around in circles, I could hear the tram running, but couldn't find my way to it. By now I was underneath it, in a series of under-ground arches and car parks, and panic had begun to set in, it was quiet and deserted, and fears that I was lost, fears that I was a women alone in a strange place, and the compelling voice , 'Go home run , run now' echoed in my head.

Tearful and confused I wandered about trying to get my bearings, becoming more and more disorientated. I have no idea how long I was lost for, my heart thudded in my chest my throat was dry and my breath didn't seem to reach my lungs. The distress brought me close to tears, like a fearful child I had no idea what to do, I couldn't think logically enough to get myself out of the mess I now found myself in.

I don't know how long I had been wondering about, I had left the hotel about eight o'clock. I didn't carry a watch and now I wandered in a daze, I had lost my sense of time. It was as if I had just switched off from my panic and had become numb. Then another odd event happened, out of the blue, leaving me feeling like some sort of miracle had happened, out of nowhere there before me, I saw a concrete ramp leading upwards in front of me.

Hope replaced the numbness, and logic stepped in, if I could get on a higher level I thought   I would be able to work out where I was. I quickly headed up the ramp and made my ascent, feelings of relief coupled with new hope and then utter anger at myself, for being so silly and getting all worked up. I emerged from the ramp exit and found myself facing the door of the G Mex Centre; the decision had been made for me.

I was relieved to be back in familiar surroundings, I must
have been wandering for over two hours, as the center didn't
open till ten o'clock, and was now very busy, within the waves
of my relief, a voice still kept telling me to run away.
I knew spirit wanted me to go back to the G Mex, so I did as
they wanted. The energies felt very different to the day before
it wasn't as bustling and seemed to take on a more relaxed and
calmer feeling.
My panic and fear quelled, but the voice which still told me to
run still gave me waves of panic and anxiousness.
I wandered around looking for gifts to take home for my
children. Looking up, I noticed an old man I had seen in the
café the day before, I knew then that I needed to speak to him,
but didn't have the faintest idea why.
I found him stood at the Arthurian Society stand, they believe
in alien connection and aspects of healing, at that time I didn't
understand although it resonated with me. They are now the
Inner Potential Centre. I recommend their books and CDs, not
just for spiritual growth but also for general interest,
I approached the stranger with total confidence; and without
any hint of nervousness at all.
I told him about myself, about the initiation, quickening and
aspects that concerned me about my situation. He listened
intently then thought for a moment and replied, 'My daughter
was like you; you have a foot in each world.'
As we talked he asked questions then told me to follow a
healing path. Then as he knew more about me he said I should
choose between teaching and medium-ship. I could do one or
the other but not both. I didn't realise at the time in solving one
problem he had given me another.
To choose my path!
So I had a foot in each world. It seemed so obvious once he
had told me. Why didn't I think of it? Such a simple answer
had solved so many problems for me. He also told me to write

a detailed letter to him in London. I felt so much lighter, and positive I felt everything that had happened in the last twenty-four hours was worth it, getting lost, the events in my hotel room, it all seemed worthwhile now, and if asked would I do it again if I knew the outcome. It would be a definite yes.

I would have also had a peep in to the hotel room at the night time activities, as I am now curious to know what had been happening.

The second day was coming to an end at the G Mex and as I wondered around I saw the man in black. He sat alone looking tired and worn out, I had no intention of going to him, but found myself doing just that.

I apologised for my nervousness the day before, I also knew that the crucifix was protection for him and his family.

I relayed the previous day's message I had without any difficulties.

As the evening events at the G Mex drew to a close, I set off for the metro Line, to start my journey home. This time I walked straight to it without getting lost and on to the train station where I had seen my friend off home the evening before. I stood waiting on the platform feeling quite happy. Then as I stood waiting, I felt something changed I couldn't quite understand why. I had the strong feeling, I was in fact on the wrong platform; my panic was such I looked for an attendant to confirm where the Newark train departed from, he was quite clear in his directions, and shock was replaced by logic, ' No it goes from over there..' He said sending me across to the other side of the station.

I sat on the other platform, still feeling something was wrong, finding myself becoming colder and colder, I didn't feel quite right and I wasn't able to put my finger on it.

The evening started to draw in and darkness and cold autumn air was sweeping into the station, a number of trains came and went commuters filed passed me, I asked passerby's as each

train came, if this was the train to Newark. Always the
same reply 'No' my heart would sink, I so wanted to go home.
I began to feel lost and vulnerable as the coldness began to bite
deep and trains continued to come and go, I found myself
waiting for an hour and a half as darkness fell.
I then asked another attendant if I was on the right platform, he
told me I wasn't and sent me back to where I had come from
across the station. I had missed my train, then I had to wait for
yet another hour and the odd feeling I had earlier had gone.
I reprimanded myself for self-doubt.
Eventually I reached Newark late on a Sunday night and found
there were no taxis or buses. I had no option but to ring Sue
and her boyfriend.
Thankfully they answered the phone and arranged my rescue.
I was told to wait by the video shop for collection, I waited in
the cold and dark, becoming uneasy as a woman alone, and
aware that I was attracting unwanted attention. The pubs began
to empty their drinkers onto the streets. Some passerby
thought I was a lady of the night. I had difficulty shaking off
one young man, he told me his girlfriend was forty, and was
carrying his child and he was twenty four. He suggested I could
go home with him. However, I eventually convinced him that I
wasn't in need of his assistance and I was truly waiting for my
friends. With a sigh of relief on my side, I watched him go on
his way a bit wobbly and worse for wear, from the nights
drinking. I then asked the time of a passerby, who I sensed
thought I was going to ask him something else, he thought I
was going to offer services.
It was by now well past ten thirty; my friends should have been
here. I looked over my shoulder at the video shop it was
Sunday night and it was closed, nothing unusual in that, I
looked at the shop more carefully.
Horror struck me it wasn't just closed but shut down, it had
relocated across town.

Panic struck me yet again for the third time that day; I set off
and ran across town as fast as my little legs would carry me
gasping for breath, the cold harsh air stinging in my lungs.
I ran out of the precinct into the main road, only to see Sue's
boyfriend driving away in the distance, I jumped up and down
in the road waving franticly hoping he would see me, but he
showed no signs of stopping.
A lump rose in my throat, my heart beat so hard, with despair
and exertion I felt it would wallop its way out of my chest.
I looked towards the direction I would have to walk; it was six
miles through dark lonely roads and lanes, to home.
Again thoughts of my safety, welled up in my mind, I started
walking preparing myself for the road ahead, glancing behind
me hoping against hope that he would return and pick me up.
I began to feel cross with myself for not making prior
arrangements to get home, how stupid I had been in general
over the whole weekend, what a fool I had made of myself
delivering a single message. Sitting on a window sill all night,
getting lost leaving my hotel, and not trusting my own
judgment about the train, and now the danger I had put myself
in.
As the traffic lights changed from green to red I started my
long walk. I looked to see if it was safe to cross then there, In
the gloom I saw the shape of a large four by four looming in
the distance was it him, 'Yes, Yes....' I thought, and once
again I flapped my arms around so much to catch his attention,
it's a wonder I didn't become airborne.
He came to a stop and I climbed in, the heat of the cab greeting
me like a mother's arms, the relief that I was now safe, made
everything that had happened seem like a bad dream.
He said he had glanced in the mirror and had just spotted me,
but he then had to find somewhere to turn around.
I was rescued and very thankful the day was over, the past
months had been quite an adventure.

My task was now complete and I could move forward on my spiritual journey.

Back home in the warmth and safety of `Highfields', I welcomed my bed and snuggled down under the duvet, and propped myself up on my most welcome pillows, feeling a sense of relief and satisfaction, and also allowing the wonder and excitement of everything that had happened, determined not to allow the negative parts of my adventure to dampen my excitement. I began to write the events of the weekend. My thoughts and feelings, filtering into the nib of my pen, as I scribbled my adventure as fast as I could in my diary. Trying to recall all that was said and all that I could remember clearly, in my senses, memory and thoughts. I had gone with so many problems whirring around in my head like and hamster on a wheel, and returned with so many more different problems solved within seven simple words.

'You have a foot in each world'!

I was very keen to write to the man in London, at last I thought there was going to be someone I could talk to, a mortal to guide me and I would be able to ask questions and receive answers. I wouldn't have to question my sanity because these people were not dead; they were alive and kicking and knew all about people like me.

With the excitement of a child, my thoughts and feelings filled my whole being, the weekend events drifting into my dreams, thoughts of my letter to London, what would I say? How would it start my letter? And at last, a stranger that had a daughter like me. I had so many questions to ask. Why did I have these abilities? How could I help man kind and mother earth? How can I reach my potential? What am I supposed to do with all

these spiritual gifts? I drifted away in my thoughts of the
last few days, until I fell asleep.

The next opportunity I had I sat down at my computer,
switched it on, located ῾Word' and presented myself with a
blank page, that in its self was an achievement as I was new to
the world of computers.
I laugh at myself now, I used to get into such a panic, if I
dusted some ones computer while cleaning houses, and up
popped the screen saver, thinking I had touched something I
shouldn't. Now all those years later, I now get into a panic
when they crash or I cannot access something, I would be lost
without it.
What's more I never thought I would ever be able to use one.
(I'm having a victor Meldrew moment 'I don't believe it'…).

So settling down with one finger poised for action, like a
woodpecker choosing the rights spot to peck, with hopeful
thoughts that the man from the Arcturian society in London
would read my letter and then help me. 'Here goes' I had all
the words in my head I knew what I wanted to say, However,
once again things would not be made easy for me, it's a simple
thing to write a letter, Yes!
So should have been delivering the message, the world of spirit
must have known I would have lost my nerve, as they had me
write the message for the man in black, prior to delivery with
no difficulties on the computer.
I began to type one finger at a time, and then as I wrote my
letter the words from my previous sentence disappeared.
Again and again I tried but the computer wasn't having any of
it; a string of problems began, as one problem occurred it was
swiftly followed by another.

So with a fuddled head, I decided, I would give up for the night making my plans to try again when I got home the next day.

The next day the computer was still not having any of it, and at one point turned its self of.

I was not about to give up. My stubborn streak kicked in, I didn't have computer six months earlier, and if modern technology wouldn't work, I still had hands, and so I decided to go back to the good old fashioned way.

As I put my eager pen to paper the room became so full of spirits, it was like Piccadilly Station, the temperature of the room dropped drastically, and I wrapped myself up in several layers of clothing, resorting to a blanket to top it all off, trying to write my letter from a gap within the folds of fabric.

I complained at spirit saying 'I didn't mind them being there, and asking them why they couldn't bring warmth instead of cold'

I started to write, and as I did so, It wasn't long before my mind kept going blank, then I felt dizzy, I tried to stop the dizziness in my head and carried on determined that I was going to write to Roger in London.

My sixth Chakra (the third eye Chakra situated on the forehead) began to spin so fast the dizziness won me over.

I could not focus on my page and I had to lay-down, in spite of my determination, my letter writing had stopped, they had won this round.

Grumbling to myself and making secret plans in my head, I was not going to be beaten; I wanted help from the living, and help from the living I was going to have. I had called war upon Spirit, and in my naivety, I would win this battle.

So over a period of two weeks I attempted many times to write my story and get it to Roger the man in London, with the Arthurian society. I realised that writing wasn't going to work.

Spirit was adamant I was not going to contact him and they did everything they could to stop me.

I was so, frustrated as in order to grow I believed I needed help from the living; in realty it was the feeling of loneliness in my unseen world that pushed this need to have a living teacher.

Then one day whilst I was working at one of the house cleaning contracts, the answer to my problem seem to appear by a stroke of luck.

The house owner was clearing out cupboards, 'Is, this any good to you?' he asked

As I saw what he was offering me, my eyes felt like they had suddenly grown stalks, like on cartoons films, he then handed me a cassette tape recorder; ha-ha I thought, smugly.

'Yes please' I promptly took the tape recorder from him thinking, this would assist me in my scheming plans, problem sorted.

Rodger in London would have a tape of my story, or perhaps sprits were making it easier for me to tell him of my adventures.

At this point I could say 'Or so I thought'

I was used to using a tape recorder, as my Grandmother always liked recording us singing as children. Feeling rather self-satisfied and smug, I called at a shop on my way home and purchased some cassette tapes.

On getting home with an air of haughtiness, I settled myself down in the bedroom and set about recording my story to send to Rodger in London. I did the one, two three tests, yes every-thing was fine, 'That's great' I thought and set about recording my letter to Rodger. However spirit had other ideas once again. Each time I recorded my letter; there was strong interference on playback, crackling and shuffling type noises, or strange unexplainable sounds. The faults didn't stop there; it also had sections of the recording missing. Thinking it was a fault on the

recorder I taped other things, like songs and talking, bird
song traffic sounds from the window, to test it. The play back
was fine no interference or blank patches; perfect recordings.
I think it is safe to say my sulking childlike lip was probably
two inches wide; by this time I knew that spirit didn't want me
to contact Rodger, and me being stubborn; instead of asking
why, and trusting the process. I was single-minded.
I was not going to be beaten, so I then planned and schemed, I
then tried outwitting spirit driving to fields, lay-bys and other
people's houses, with piles of spare batteries, to enable me to
make my recording.
But to no avail. On one occasion I drove twenty miles away
then started my recording; it took spirit a total of twenty
minutes before they caught up with me and distorted the tape
recording, yet again.
Now being a Pisces born on the cusp of Aires in the year of the
rat, I have a very determined streak in me.
I say like a ferret hanging on a finger, and I was hanging on to
my need to have a mortal guide so I didn't feel so alone.
I so wanted to see a person's lips moving their eye contact and
feelings within the voice of someone living.
Not just responding to a voice in my head; that left me
questioning things constantly. Was it my voice, or Spirit?
Am I sane or going insane? Eventually spirit must have
realised I was not going to give up, they relented and I wrote
my sixteen page letter, wrapped in a blanket with one lone
large cold Spirit hanging over my shoulder.
As I addressed and stamped my letter I knew in my heart even
at that point it would never reach Roger. But hope springs
eternal, I posted it, I felt the letter slip from my fingers and
heard the tap as it dropped into the bottom of the letter box,
still sensing it would not reach him. Hoping against hope
Spirit would relent and give me the thing I thought I wanted the
most, a live mortal guide.

As I suspected I never did get a reply and six weeks later I
knew I never would.
The feelings of disappointment, and loneliness swept over me
yet again and I slipped into a childlike lonely sulk.
At this time I began to accept and know that the world of spirit
had plans in mind for me; and me being me I just didn't realise.
It wasn't until I found myself on a family trip that I didn't even
want to go on, with my x husband and our children.

A couple of weeks later I found myself on a trip to Loch Ness
in the Highlands of Scotland, with my son and daughter, the
children buzzed about and my son was very keen to find the
monster that lay in the deep dark waters of the loch, probably
intent on adding it to his menagerie, and was quite
disappointed that he didn't get to see it in person.
My daughter had already seen the gift shop on the way in, and
like any ten year old girl that was far more interesting than an
elusive monster. The lock is the largest and deepest expanse of
inland water in the UK.
As we walked around the Centre in Drumnadrochit, I gave the
children a handful of pennies to throw into the wishing well.
And more as a memory from my own childhood with my
grandmother and my mum, who gave me penny's for the
wishing wells. I saved one back for myself and hovered by the
well, Not wanting some other adult to think I was being foolish
if they saw what I was about to do.
The children had now dashed off in the direction of the gift
shop. If the real `Nessy' wouldn't show himself; they were
content to have a green fluffy one in its place.
As I passed the well I casually threw the penny into the water
and made a wish.

Asking for some people like me to come into my life, not for one moment expecting any come back from my childish act. Spirit was listening to my plea, my saddened heart and despair was growing. Like any parent with a child they love, the world of spirit wants you to have those things that are in your best interest, and for your highest good. And where able will oblige, they will give you want you need not what you think you need. I asked for someone like me to enter my life......three weeks later my wish came true!

A phone call from my tutor, were I hard trained in my early therapy's rang me to tell me my reflexology certificate was ready for collection, with in his messages of congratulation's well done, I went into a self-worth panic of 'I don't know how to do it, I can't do it' I spluttered, and no matter how he tried to convince me I had past my exam's, nothing he could say would assure me that I could do reflexology. So he told me I could join his new class of trainee reflexologists, and sit in the classes for free, to increase my confidence. Just to make me see that I could in fact do reflexology. At that time I was so lacking in confidence and in my own abilities, so different from the person I am now.
There in the class I met Brenda, Wendy and Anne; as soon as I saw them I knew we were like minded people: and they realised that I was one of them.
A few weeks later I was asked to join their healing group in St Annes in Nottingham, and the odd thing is I was so thrilled to think, I was to be with other people like me, I didn't get afraid of driving in the town, something that had been a real problem for me previously.
I was well aware my wish at Loch Ness had come true; and consequently this opened the door to the next stage of my

development, and strengthened my trust in the world of spirit, they were listening to me after all.

Growth and Transformation

Here I leave the story temporally to give you some guidance on the spiritual path.

On any spiritual path growth is necessary, lessons have to be learned mistakes made; repeating patterns over and over, until we identify our actions and become more self- aware of how actions have consequences for us or others. If necessary, making adjustment to our life, not just in spiritual practices but life's experiences too.

If you are going to walk a spiritual path, you need several tools in your toolbox, to start with, these tools won't cost you a penny; they are simply, trust, faith, belief, love and confidence in the universal life force and spirits that guide you, confidence in yourself and your own abilities, without allowing ego to have its way with you.

Ego, this is a big obstacle to overcome, and causes so many issues including slowing down or stopping of spiritual development, it can hinder you, by attracting the wrong kinds of people to you, in some cases other people will avoid you. Identifying you have an ego is a good thing, getting on top of it is another, and much more difficult to deal with.

I have met many people whose ego have or are stunting their growth, or indeed stopped it. Sometimes their ego is so big they don't even notice, and others who I have gently but calmly tried to allow them to reach their own conclusion, it's not about what you have done for someone, how many past lives you have had, were your soul is from, how much training you have received, the energy's you channel, or how many people you have helped, it's just about helping and doing for doings sake, unconditionally and expecting no reward, other than your heart knowing you have been unconditional in your giving.

You also need to try to be non-judgmental of other people's belief systems; this can be difficult when there harming others. Each one of us is a unique individual, no two people are identical; no two people share the exact same thoughts and feelings, each of us vibrate at a particular frequency of light and sound.

Our experiences make us who we are; yes there will be similarities, such as likeminded ideas and soul energy connections.

In my opinion it does not matter what you believe in, as long as it does no harm to others. My student groups are of mixed faiths and beliefs from hedge witches, sea witches, spiritualists, angelic, alien Catholic's, Buddhists, Christian's, Shamans, and some that are exploring all avenues, however they all have made a decision that there is more to life.

The spiritual pathway is not an easy one; you may find yourself starting out like I did with a foot in both worlds; logic and psyche have their own agenda, amongst you living your normal daily life. With logic and psyche having a private battle of their own with yours truly stuck in the middle.

Having a foot in each world causes all kinds of confusion, anger, frustration, pain, joy, wonder, and the constant nagging question that logic likes to throw in, 'Your mad, crazy a bail short of a full load, a prawn less on a cocktail' Logic telling you, 'It's your imagination, fantasy, infatuation' and much more, then in pops the psyche yet again,

'Well how did you know about that then?'

Reminding you of incidents and events you could not possibly have known about previously.

In comes logic not about to be defeated, a favorite word to explain so many events is 'It's coincidence, there just happens to be a few together....they happen all the time' and then in comes the psyche again with its opposing argument.

I know I keep going on about the first book I read, and here
it is again, and now you understand the foot in each world
scenario, you can appreciate why the passage in Lillian Becks
book 'Into the light' says, 'Few are rarely able to handle it and
become unstable'

I have come across people who have become unstable and lost
their balance, it's easy to write everything off as Spirit.

For example, things go missing, the lights keep flickering or
bulbs blowing, electrical appliances keep breaking, the TV
turns its self on and off at will, candles flickering, ask yourself
logical questions first, are there any drafts, loose wires, inferior
bulbs, rule out all logical avenues before you blame spirit.

Retrace your steps, where did I leave the lost item? Were you
tired when I put them down etc, are there electrical circuit
problems such as power surges and so on.

When you have exhausted the logical, then look at the possible
spiritual reasons.

As you develop you will able to sense the difference between
life's everyday happenings and Spirit intervening.

I have seen many cases were people have called me in blaming
spirit, when sometimes it has been dangerous electric's or
those moments of absent mindedness we all get from time to
time.

Now when you have eventually come to terms with the fact
you are not a fruit loop, going mad, and the men in white coats,
are not going to get a bag of jelly baby's to lure you in to
getting in to the shiny black van, asking you to wear the nice
padded jacket with sparkling buckles that fasten at the back.
To take you away and lock you up upon on some far distant
shore, throwing away the key.

Your spiritual growth will accelerate! In leaps and bounds, until you come to the stage where your tired brain says Whoa! Stop! And you try to filter through your mind all that has happened and is happening.

I recommend to my students to try keeping a Spiritual Diary, or if you are of Pagan leanings it is called `A Book of Shadows,' it will help for you to keep a track of some of the amazing events that occur, which may not seem too relevant at the time, it will also show you how far you have come in such a short space of time.

Stick to spiritual happenings rather than it being a daily diary that is kept about life in general. If however, there is an underling theme linked to the spiritual then include it, if it feels to be a part of your growth then it belongs in the diary.

It doesn't have to be pages and pages, for example key words, as reminders or a signpost is all that you need. For example the note I made about the ladies in the car park, letting me know that was how to get to Manchester, or the book in the library window. It could be a voice, a gut feeling, instinct, for example you thought of someone then bumped into them unexpectedly while out or they rang you, you knew something was going to happen and it did, etc, write down any event or thought you think links to your spiritual growth, including visions, dreams meditations and any experience in classes.

It may not even seem or mean much at the time; however it may be a thread in a chain of events that are in the forming, like my own experiences and dreams.

That almost eighteen years later lead to where I am now.

Over the years you will be surprised at all you will have done and experienced, if writing is a problem then you could use a digital recorder or tape, whatever is easiest for you and remember to date them. As your growth accelerates, it brings new experiences, and you will find your intuition sharpens, and realizations dawns, when you have accepted that it will take

more than half a pound of jelly babies to get you to climb
in the van with the nice men, who plan to take you away.
You can move forward with more calmness and balance, and
learn how to integrate it into your life for your own and others
benefit.

At this point in my development, a quickening took place.
I had come to terms with what was happening in my life, I
knew I wasn't mad and so I began to trust Spirit with more
depth of understanding, even though it was a number of years
before I trusted myself.
With the new found belief and trust in the universal life force
along with all its facets, I now found my Spiritual growth
progressed faster; it was thankfully less of a bumpy ride as I
grew, well for a short while any way!
The issue of a foot in each world, had given me more than its
fair share of problems, the constant arguing between psyche
and logic was physically and mentally draining, it lead to me
many sleepless nights, feelings of exhaustion, and that constant
nagging logic giving me a prod and telling me, I was in fact
mad after all, and I was by now starting to experience the
feelings of being ill.
I was being drained by unseen forces that were not of light,
added to my own exhaustion caused by mental stress and
physical fatigue from working so hard.
I was questioning everything over and over again; added to
this, I was hounded by individual living energy vampires that
drained me and left me feeling weak, I was now meeting those
living individuals who make you feel like they had left a sticky
invisible residue of negativity all over you. (I will talk about
energy vampires in a later chapter.)

Sometimes you will also find some spirits are keen for you to work before you are ready, and a few of those popped in among the mixture of spirits that had my best interest at heart, and believe me some spirits will use you twenty four seven if given the chance, without any consideration for your health. If you don't put a stop to it you will end up joining them sooner than you should.

Asking for a guide to help control who comes in and out of your aura (this is the energy field that surrounds your body, more on this later)

To control those spirits who don't have your best interests at heart, normally they're normal earth bound spirits just wanting to help, but are not aware of the rules or if they are, they want to help so much they forget we are human channels.

To deal with the influx of spirit demands, I created two rooms inside my mind, I would visualize the Spirits waiting in one room and my guide checking who could come in and when, and this guide is called a gate keeper

Then we would help the spirits in order of need in the time allotted. If spirit wants you to work, and you're too tired, and it's not urgent, it is ok to ask them to wait.

Time is not an issue when working in the normal world of Spirit, or general soul rescue of this type.

It can be an issue when working at an advanced level.

One thing to note is,

Growth is a spiritual battle and you are a Spiritual Warrior!

One day a Spirit once told me, 'We feel sad, as so many people give up, or who have turned away from us when they are almost there, many fall at the last hurdle with the winning post in their sight'

I can understand why this happens, I have been challenge by spirits who did not want me to walk this path; the challenges may become less as you reach a more advanced level in your development However if negative energies are nibbling at you

it is because they are trying to find a way to stop your
progress and that sometimes happens when you are about to do
something for the world of light spirit, that will have a greater
impact for the light, the bigger the nibble from negative
energy's, you can be sure you're going to have a bigger effect.
It's not an easy path to take, temptation constantly nipping at
your heals,
'Give it up' a voice would say; Life would be so much easier
without all this confusion' and the negative spirits will also
offer you everything you can desire, from been rich and
healthy to fulfilling the dream you always wanted.
If you give in, remember the pleasure will more than likely
have its roots in the world of ego and the material world, it will
be short lived, the happiness will be temporary and there's
often a high price to pay which they normally don't tell you
about.
I knew if I had have given in to the negative energies, it would
feel as though life would be easier, no more arguing with
myself just go to work do what I had to do and live a material
life. For me personally I could not do that, I felt like I would
be letting God down (for me God energy is the whole universe,
with all its realms)
So there I was like a ferret on a finger hanging on, and no
matter how hard it gets, you hang in there.
The rewards are worth it in the end.
Also as I said earlier we are not all the same, every-ones path is
different, depending on what resonates with you and what
doesn't.
There are so many paths you can walk, and in so many ways,
which way you will go? How you develop? And what you
will grow into? It all depends on you, the choices you make.
What you like and what you don't like, how much you want
this path, a little, a lot or whole heartedly.

Also, don't be afraid to change your direction or adapt it at times.

I have met people who have been trained in such a way that is considered pure and that is beautiful and they cannot deviate from that training, and in some cases it is true, as the old ways must be remembered.

However our planets vibrations have changed with the onset of 12.12.2012, so some things will change. It is up to you to identify if that ridged structure, can also restrict your growth. As an example I was told by Roger in London, 'you, can't do healing and teaching, and be a medium at the same time; you have to choose' It wasn't the case for me. I was told by someone, I couldn't work with Reiki and channel spirit at the same time, however Reiki is energy and spirit is energy they work well together, and at the end of the day spirit drives the bus you are just the conductor.

Whatever way someone chooses to work, you will find if they are working from the heart, what they deliver is through the guidance of Spirit.

It is spirit, who knows what is best for you and your path, in respect of skills, missions and task.

You will find over time you will have a spiritual tool box, think of reiki as one spanner, healing as another spanner, soul rescue another etc.

I compare myself to an empty cardboard toilet tube, I know it's an odd analogy to use, but this is me, a toilet tube is just a bit of cardboard, which hold the paper together, is simple and basic, no frills no fanfare. Whatever a person needs flows through it; to who or whatever, it`s between the receiver and the source; it`s not me! As I said earlier 'Spirit drives this bus' I'm just the conductor."

The spiritual growth pattern of everyone varies greatly, and what you grow into is just as varied. For example imagine yourself taking a box full of mixed seeds, now scatter them on

to the ground, water them and wait for them to grow; which one will you be? How big will you grow? How many other seeds will fall from your faded flower head?
These will in turn, grow into more and more plants.
Mary watered the seed in me in those early years; I started to grow, fed by lessons, knowledge, and experiences, doors within doors were opened for me and here I am.
I hope as you read my story I am opening a door for you too by sharing my thoughts and words, and I hope your journey will be as fruitful as mine.
You will never stop growing and learning. I'm still growing, and in turn I pass on my knowledge and experiences to others. Many of whom are now on their own spiritual path, some passing their knowledge and skills onto others.
You could say watering the seeds in them, and yes with effort and willingness it will grow. Some will grow a little, some whole heartedly, some will be blown away by the wind and never grow, there will be others that rest beneath the snow waiting for the thaw. Some will stunt their own growth, others will buzz around like a bee from flower to flower, some will unfortunately, never grow.
When you walk the spiritual path you are not only helping yourself, you are also helping individual people, you are helping the whole of humanity to rise there vibrations to be in union with mother earth and the planetary systems, you are aiding all individuals in the next transition of the human development.
Living the spiritual life has its rewards, and consequently it spreads throughout the world, bringing love, peace, healing, happiness, knowledge, balance, wholeness, and experience's you could only dream about, plus a feeling of belonging, and feelings of pure pleasure.
For a moment just imagine sitting in a bright light and an angel pacing their hands upon you, or imagine someone giving you

love like you have never experienced, it that simple and the feelings are beyond joy, they are pure bliss and bliss is a very different feeling to anything you may have experienced, it goes beyond the physical planes to a world I hope you many of you will experience.

Spiritual growth will also bring changes within your life, so be prepared. Some changes may not be what you expected or even pleasant, you may even experience the end of relationships; it could be your husband, or partner, friends or family, as you outgrow them and move forwards.

Also, you may change your thoughts and feelings about a number of things that resonated with you in the past; they no longer are suitable or relevant to you now.

If that happens, and it feels for your highest good or it feels right in your heart, to let people go then do so.

Perhaps it may be because you have made change they are then free to grow themselves, may be you were holding them back. And in setting them free the wind will be beneath their wings, they may not be of a spiritual nature, however spirit are still in their lives and will always try to help them too.

Some life times may not always be about higher spiritual growth it could be life's lessons, or karma and often a mixture of both.

The list of scenarios and possibilities on the spiritual adventure are endless. If you really want to grow in mind and spirit you will know instinctively what is for your highest good.

So whether you grow into a mighty oak or a daisy, please remember each of you has a special part to play in this world. Trust the process, events will happen in a way that's timely to your growth, and you need not worry about missing the watering can. When you're ready and willing to grow 'Your time will come'

Whatever your feelings whether your goal is planetary peace, enlightenment, self- awareness, or raising the vibration of the planet; you will learn there are many ways of working and many quests to work for. It is up to you how you proceed and how far you take it. It`s your choice how you wish to work. It`s your path on which you walk, Spirit will guide you and open doors in some cases, giving you a push through, or a swift kick up the backside if it is so needed.

When I moved to Highfields in 1998 I looked up to the heavens and I made a promise to help those that are living, those that are dying and those that are already dead.

Before I too die and make my transition, or as I say return home.

That was a long time ago and my personal choice, a promise! It was only ten years ago I realised how bigger promise I committed to. I do not for one moment have any regrets, this life it suites me fine and I am happier with my spiritual life, than I could ever have imagined, being in service to the light and the many avenues of working for different light beings is an honor and a privilege, I feel humble to be considered worthy.

There have been, personal sacrifices, I'm sure there will be more; even so I trust Spirit totally. And even at the level of growth I am I still some times pull on teddy's ears like a child, they whisper patience and trust.

When events have become clear, I feel a little childish and apologise words whispering 'You are in human form, it's to be expected'

Over the early years I learnt how to identify the Light Spirits from the dark ones even though they can hide.

Recognising the dark one tricks and hiding places comes over time and with practice. (My book 'Phoenix in the shadows' will cover the darker aspects of negative energy)

If you are not sure about a spirit visitor, ask your divine source or angels or use whatever you feel safe and secure with, to guide you as to the right action in that particular situation. Remember the Lord's Prayer, is one of the most powerful vibrational verses to drive the Dark Spirits or negative energy away.

I personally have handed a lot over to the world of Spirit, and in the last few years my life, which was my choice.

If you should choose to do the same, they will guide as much as you wish them to, one of the spiritual laws is that. 'They cannot interfere in your life' it is your life not there's. So if you want spirit to help you, you have to ask. Weather you choose to take there guidance is also up to you.

Nevertheless, remember no Spirit of Light will force you against your will, or tell you to do things which will harm others or yourself.

Many of you made a choice before you were reincarnated in this life, to learn life lessons, heal karma, or work for the universal life force, or to bring a particular vibration to earth in order to aid her healing, you may even be here to carry out a range of tasks.

Whatever you decide to do, it is your personal adventure that will be like the ever shifting desert sands, and remember the future is not set in stone. It took a long time for me to find my path, as I read my old diaries when I began this book, I realise it was only sixteen years ago that I began to grow.

So much has happened in those years, so much personal growth so many Spiritual occurrences even those that felt like nothing less than a miracle. I had forgotten about so much, the diaries have been a reminder, numerous notes on bits of paper and even till receipts all stored here and there.

As the spiritual events flow in and out of my daily life it feels so natural like a daily habit, like cleaning your teeth or going to work, even breathing.

For me it is a part of the normal daily routine. When this happens spiritual events can easily be forgotten.

Furthermore you may find yourself spending more time in the spiritual world than the material and this can cause problems. I must admit I was often in that frame of mind.

When you are for example spending too much time wrapped within the spirit world, for example too much talking to spirit, or journeying at this point you will have some life event, a reminder given to you, for example a practical life event may happen eg, a burst pipe, or a breakdown of some kind, Remember the afterlife comes after life and the material world is also a learning plane.

You need to be aware that the world of healing, spirit, and all its facets, in which it presents itself, should be respected. Always sacred and special, no matter how small an event, you should never take it for granted, or take for granted your ability to give others healing etc you should never misuse the spiritual energy given to you to try to create something that is not appropriate or influence an outcome. If you need help in a situation, simply project light energy, and let spirit do their work, often they will guide you to right action.

Most of all don't become focused on yourself with words I am, look at me, I helped him / her so I should be rewarded or be of an egotistical mind. In the spiritual life we give unconditionally from the heart.

Remember if you are working for the light, you are merely a channel. An empty cardboard tube out of a toilet roll, the energy simply flows through you from the source of light; you will have your own views and thoughts on what your source of light is.

Learning to keep the tube clear so the flow of light energy from the source is another lesson and being willing to keep the tube clear, in order to allow spirit to do their work is yet another skill to be learned. The old phrase of been an empty vessel so you can be filled comes to mind here.

Spending a Penny

Now I will continue with my adventure and take you back to
the event at Loch Ness and the penny casually thrown into the
wishing well, without any real expectation, as I mentioned
earlier about small miracles this was surely one of those.

A wish came true for me and I was invited to restart my
reflexology class and met Anne Brenda and Wendy. Who ran
the development group.

I even found I was brave enough to drive into the outskirts of
St Annes, in Nottingham to the group. As I mentioned earlier
driving was not a confident skill of mine and one which I
didn't really like in large built up areas particularly towns.

At this point of third editing I live in the center of Nottingham
city. A city, I have avoided for thirty years and wouldn't even
drive there, another miracle, and the question on my lips to
spirit know is why I am here in this city.

Anne, Wendy, Brenda and Vera, were now my friends and for
the first time since my spiritual development began, I had not
just one mortal guide but four. At last I wasn't alone, and here
within the healing group/circle, I was given the protection and
watered by their knowledge like a daisy in a plant pot, growth
was certain.

Members of the group guided me with their experiences and
knowledge, and they gave me the opportunity to grow allowing
my own spiritual abilities to continue to develop, in my own
way and also a safe and protected environment. It wasn't long
before I found myself sharing messages and healing with them.
On the other hand for me personally I began also to share with
Spirit, at a much deeper level, allowing Spirits' to enter my
body within the safety and protection of the more experienced
group members. I remember the first Spirit sharing, feeling
their gentle pressure and push as the Spirit slipped into my

Aura. I would then feel their stature as they were in life, their emotions and feelings.

At first the Spirit's that shared with me, allowed me just to sense and feel. I sensed the changes in my body; I'm five foot three inches in height, so for me the feelings of a small women or becoming the stature of a large man was strange at first. Sensing being someone old or young or from a different racial background and culture was quite inspiring.

Sometimes it was like history coming back alive. Imagine feeling the weight of amour pressing against your chest, or the heaviness of a Tudor gown, the scaring on the face of a Massi warrior, the feelings of being a native Indian, the height and the shape of the nose, the tightness of the skin stretched over your cheek bones.

It wasn't always something so grand, it had other sides too, An old lady's with severe arthritis in the fingers and my own hand felt has hers had been, crumpled and twisted, or a man with a broken fore-arm who had died here in England and wanted to go home, a young man killed on a motor bike gave me the feeling of a broken shoulder, a victim of car accident, just mentioning a few.

A momentary glimpse of other people's lives, sharing the history of the past, it was an incredible feeling.

Although, not without risk.

I met those in the Spirit World who helped the living and the dead; and I experienced many people from different cultures and backgrounds and different times in history over the years. The thing to remember, time and travel are not a problem for those in the Spirit World, as they slip easily from plain to plain. A skill which with time and practice, and many years later I too found myself able to slip from plain to plain of existences.

You must also be aware it takes time for those that are newcomers in the Spirit World to learn how to use energy to make you aware of their presence and to manifest themselves and communicate with us on the this side. It takes time to learn and adapt, so Spirit too learn in their new world how to manipulate energy.

A group energy acts like a beacon of light to those in the Spirit World, they come offering help and advice, or alternatively are just attracted by the glow of energy created. It can also attract those Spirits that are lost or not of light so protection is a vital part of working in this field, as those who are dark may wish to cause some disruption, this topic is covered in my book , 'Phoenix in the shadows'

There were also many things that I had never told the group. I confess in the early days I did play my cards very close to my chest at first, and I was guilty of putting my spiritual companions in this world and the next to the test. I had been convinced for so long that maybe I was not of sound mind or so logic would have me believe. I was always told I was gullible and easily led, so I was determined to make sure this would not be the case.

Vera who was a visiting medium was aware that I needed someone to control who came in and out of my Aura, as I said in the beginning I was better run in than a number sixty five bus, so it was decided that I should be given a Gate Keeper. This was done by giving me a Spirit Guide who would control who was allowed in my Aura, the gate keeper would sort out why they were visiting and who would have to wait their turn, and how urgent the situation was. This is the time when I created the two rooms inside my mind.

Until that time, I allowed Spirits to come and go in and out of my aura as they please.

I felt sorry for them and wanted to help them all. I didn't want to hurt their feelings, by saying no. Much to my own cost of ill health, sleepless nights I did learn to say you will have to wait, or to say no.

Later on in my mind, the two areas I had created for the
Spiritual work became one for rescue and one for other
matters, quite a simple structure, really and it worked well.
I slept better, my health and energy levels improved, and the
heaviness on my shoulders lightened considerably.

Amongst all these goings on and the growth within the St
Annes group, I was still being told by Spirit to send light to the
man in black, although I still had no idea why it should be me.
Nevertheless I did as they asked without question and kept to
the task they had set for me. By now I had learnt to become
more balanced and able to place myself in whichever world I
was working at that particular point in time, focusing my work
to keep a much needed balance between the physical life and
the Spiritual.
About the same time, out of the blue a few weeks later I had
another dream relating to the man in black, and it became clear
that the foundations of whatever he was planning were unsafe
in some way. This point had been mentioned previously in the
first message, and it now became clear to me that it was related
to the financial foundations of a project he was to undertake.
The reference from the Bible about a man who builds his house
on sand, and the one who built his house on rock, kept coming,
into my mind. I also saw business men in suits in a meeting.
Unfortunately I never did deliver the message.

He had in fact come into my head for a totally different reason.
On the second of November, a few weeks after my adventure at
the G Mex in Manchester, I was driving to work, when
suddenly a car pulled out across the path of a another vehicle
almost causing a serious accident. I felt a wave of strong
emotions, plus sickness in the pit of the stomach, and fear.

That sort of tingling cold sweat that only occurs when you have made a serious mistake or something horrific has happened.

Although it was a near miss and I was an observer, all the emotions I was feeling felt like it was I who was involved in the event. The car who had avoided the collision had the registration 'Tim W'. Also on my car cassette the Heartland music was playing at the time. I sensed a connection and that something unpleasant had happened.

I carried on my journey to work, still feeling all the emotions from the near miss accident, I couldn't understand at the time why was I feeling all these things.

When I reached the house I was due to clean, spirit wanted me to work immediately, I wasn't sure how I could as I was there as a cleaner for four hours at this house, and cleaning two more houses after this one. Feeling a little fuddled and confused, Spirit had already taken action and my employer received an urgent telephone call and had to go out immediately, not knowing when she would be back. She scooped up her children and was gone in a matter of minutes.

I was left standing alone in the black and white tiled entrance hall, the great grandfather clock standing silent as it always did and the house seemed to become like a shell, I was surprised and bewildered. What was happening? I was aware that Spirit needed me to work, and I was still quite inexperienced at this stage of my development, and although uncertain I sensed I should put my trust in them.

I could still feel the emotions for the near miss accident. Given the immature stage of my development I realised these emotions were not in fact mine;

I then entered a visualization state quite naturally without thinking. Sitting at the top of the landing

I could see the man in black quite clearly, Spirit stepped into my mind and I followed the instructions I was being given.

Firstly, I was instructed to channel light from source and then through my own Chakra's into his, then radiating the light through the body of the man in black and connecting him directly to the light source. I felt hand to hand contact as if he was with me in person; I stayed for quite some time with my Spirit Instructors until I was told to leave. I knew the man in black, was knowledgeable enough do this himself however for whatever reason I was asked to do it for him at this time.

I have no idea what happened to him that day, maybe one day someone will tell me. I have also never been instructed to send light quite that way again.

Over the following weeks I sent healing and light as instructed morning and night, until one day a Spirit quite simply told me to stop and that I no longer need to send the energy as he no longer needed it, As usual I did as I was asked.

Some weeks later I saw him again, whilst I was in a trance state. He looked so well and happy. This time he touched his forehead in a greeting gesture, and yellow light came back to me. I returned the gesture and knew that was my task done.

Even though I now had the group in St Annes, I was still hoping that by some miracle Roger from London would still write to me after I had posted my letter to him, even though as I said I knew it would never reach him. I now came to realise in resolving one problem for me, he had left me with another. He had told me I had to choose between healing, teaching and medium-ship, he said I could not do both, and yet my way of working and training by Spirit showed me I was capable of integrating a number of methods.

Meanwhile, I continued to scribble away in my diary, trying to make sense of all that had happened and was still happening. I listed what I was able to do and how spirit had me working with my abilities, they were certainly a mixed tool box, and trying to separate them was most certainly not working. I realised at the time of final edit it was the energy's he was connected to in Rodgers group that were resonating with me. When it came down to my training, spirit had their own ideas and so I went along with their guidance. If messages came through with healing that was fine by me and if I needed to pass on teaching that was fine too.

When I give a treatment it can involve quite a combination of tools even to this day, although I no longer do the physical therapies.

It wasn't all plain sailing for me, as frequently visitors in the form of negative spirits still kept telling me that I would be far better of leaving this God thing behind.

On one occasion a rather clever one put such a lot into my mind, I suddenly found myself experiencing old patterning and conditions of past behavior that I had already outgrown a long time ago. The old irrational thoughts and feelings would well up and repeat themselves all in twenty four hours.

Many outgrown behavior patterns like worrying unnecessarily, creating problems when there wasn't really any, surfaced combined with unsettling dreams and nightmares, resulting in me fighting to wake myself up to escape the horrors.

One evening it became so bad that I found myself being attacked physically. I woke in the night to find myself being suffocated by unseen forces, hands pressed tightly over my mouth and nose, as I struggled, gasping for breath, I tried to focus my mind and control my panic. I chanted the Lord's Prayer, franticly in my head to make whatever it was and it let me go, after a struggle it released its grip. The fear left me sitting on the edge of my bed wide awake and so afraid.

I questioned myself, was it a dream or real. However, I knew it was real as I remember looking up towards the ceiling as I opened my eyes during the attack, unable to draw breath,

seeing a shadowy being, so clear to me. Knowing what
ever was attacking me was not of light and had in its way
attempted to silence me.

I do not wish to frighten you but as the saying goes 'Fore
warned is forearmed'

If anything like this happens to you, or you are afraid, chant the
Lord's Prayer or the equivalent you don't have to be a
Christian for it to work, remember it is a universal vibration
regardless of any faith, it will work.

There will also be those of you, who choose to work in the
name of light, we call world service which means working for
the universal light, mankind and mother earth, putting their
needs first.

There may be times when there is a possibility that you will
find you are under attack by negative energies. This doesn't
happen to everyone, however, the more of an impact you're
going to make in service, there is a good chance negative
energies will have a go at frightening you and attempt to
change your mind, hoping to frighten you so much; that you
will give up following your path. Negative spirits, will look for
the chink in your armor, and try to find a way in; so see if you
can find your weakness first.

(Phoenix in the Shadows; covers this in more depth.)

Remember you are a Spiritual Warrior. Your faith is your
sword and your love in the divine force by whatever name you
call it is your armor and that is more powerful than you can
ever imagine.

In general I have found that negative energies will find that
chink in your armor, and use every fear you possess, they have
even said they would kill my children and that is enough to
stop any mother in her tracks. I said, 'If that's what God says is
to be then so be it', and I place my children's care in the
divines and the light spirits hands.

On one occasion I knew of an event which would result in
my daughter funeral, I called an earth worker and a white witch
to assist me in protecting her, the instigator of the fore told
event was also worked for to prevent the future occurrence, the
use of light energy resulted, In him turning his temper on
himself causing minimal damage, and her life was saved. The
young man in question turned his life around and the end result
was positive for all concerned. As I have stated before
predictions are not always set in stone.

That in its self is a lesson in trust. I have also found negative
energies have little patience, like a spoilt child they want it and
want it now.

So that brings me to discuss Protection; it is very important to
find a way of protecting yourself from negative in all its forms,
be it from the living or the dead. Here are a few suggestions.

- ❖ The first one is the Lord's Prayer or the equivalent, as I
  said you don't have to be a Christian it works for
  everyone.
- ❖ You can visualize white light or a colour that comes
  into your mind, surround yourself.
- ❖ Some people use bubbles or egg shapes in colours,
- ❖ You can visualize yourself drawing a bright electric
  blue light around yourself, I use this also to seal a room
  at bedtime sometimes I will draw it around my bed,
  windows doors or visualize a sheet of the light so I am
  fully encased.
- ❖ You can visualize yourself wearing a suite of armor, or
  a suite that zips up over you.
- ❖ There are talismans and crystals. There are many to
  choose from, black tourmaline, or black obsidian, a
  Merkaba or a Selfic Disk from the Damanhur.
- ❖ You can use, amulets of all kinds,

- ❖ There is wand magic,(a wand doesn't hold its charge so it will need recharging before use)
- ❖ Aura soma.
- ❖ Energy sprays.
- ❖ Pagan methods such as the power ball.
- ❖ Try chanting the mantra 'OM Dum Durgar Namah Yie' this is calling out to the universal light for the goddess of protection to watch over you.
- ❖ Simply praying or chanting.
- ❖ Call a spirit ancestor that makes you feel safe
- ❖ Call in Angels, Guardians or Ancestors of light.
- ❖ If you are attuned to something like Reiki, you can use your symbols.
- ❖ Call in a Guardian Spirit Animal,
- ❖ Draw a Pentagram, you don't need to be a Pagan to do this,
- ❖ Sea or rock salt,
- ❖ Sacred water,
- ❖ White light poring over around you and through you.
- ❖ Violet flames or white flames.
- ❖ Think of Angel wings wrapping around you
- ❖ You can charge or program an item to help with protecting you, (the power of is a influential tool)
- ❖ Use a pendulum or other dowsing method to find the right protection for you.
- ❖ Sacred geometry and crystal grids
- ❖ Sacred geometry forms such as holons

There are many ways to protect yourselves these are but a few. I use a number of protections including white or violet flames, and phoenix wings to surround groups.
I will use armor when I'm within a situation where I am fighting negative forces.

Sometimes, I will have several energy items such as crystals or sacred objects which I will wear and yes ladies, a good place to store them is your bra cups, as the gentlemen have more pockets in their clothes than we have. It is a good place to keep them and also near the heart chakra, which is the bridge between the physical and the spiritual planes.

This caused quite a giggle among the goddess group, when we came to realise I was not alone with my hiding place. I trust spirit to guide me on what to use for protection.

As you develop your vibration increases and other forms of high energy protection is given.

Exploring your Options

My search for my own kind was on going. I visited many mind,
body and spirit fairs to connect to like-minded people.
Exploring other possibilities and searching for answers to my
questions.
The ever burning questions I wanted answers to, kept running
through my mind.
'Who am I?'
'Why am I like this?'
'What am I to do with it?'
And why couldn't, I talk to Roger in London?
I was Sulking and feeling alone, although I had the St Anne's
group, and even though the world of Spirit remained ever close
to me I still felt like I didn't quite fit in.

The mind, body and spirit fairs or health fairs are a good place
to start exploring your journey, you may find what you are
looking for or meet someone who will set you onto your next
stage of development. You may find an object or a book that
will feel like its jumped off the shelf at you, if possible you
should purchase the item; it's a signpost, and will give you
something to help you on your journey, even if it's just a
paragraph in a book like those I mentioned such as `Into the
Light' by Lillian Beck.
I recommend you try to visit a few fairs, they all have many
avenues for you to explore.
Some fairs will also feel more comfortable than others and
remember there are those who are not from the heart but the
pocket.
Things will be dressed up given a new name and hailed as the
latest best thing, better than everything else, when much of the
time it is an old way reinvented and given a different name and
a high price tag accompanies it.

Follow your instincts, your gut feeling, the Spiritualist in
my groups have a saying,
'First thoughts Spirits, second thoughts your own.' I have
found this to be quite accurate. Also try keeping an open mind;
you will come across things which will gel instantly with you,
other things will leave your nerves jangling or make you feel
cross. Some things will leave you completely baffled,
wondering how they can believe it. Your logic going no, I
don't think so. There will be things that you feel are completely
crazy, try not to be judgmental. Remember just because you
can't connect or agree with a particular way of working with
same energy, doesn't mean it is always wrong. It's their
personal way that works best for them, if it's from the heart it
is on the right path. No matter how strange or bazar their
workings.
We are all unique individuals; no two people are the same.
The good thing about holistic and complementary methods,
they take uniqueness into consideration. Use your intuition,
find what feels right for you, and go with it, as long as you
want to. As long as it causes no harm to others and is given
with love you can't go far wrong.
When you start to explore, you need to be aware to expect
changes, in your growth as you go along your path, you may
find something you have been working with for a long time,
doesn't feel right anymore. Don't beat yourself up over it, you
learned what you needed to, and now it's time for new growth
and moving on. Think of it as a new tool like a spanner or
hammer and put it in your spiritual toolbox.
You may find yourself changing in the complete opposite
direction or going back to something you haven't worked with
for a long time, finding you can in fact adapt it to your new
direction and enhance whatever you are working with, and
that's ok too you are on your own individual path of growth
and transformation.

When I first started out on this path, in 1998 the Reiki attunement was the first step, then a massage course which lead to aromatherapy, reflexology, and other holistic skills.

At each hurdle crossed, I thought that skill I had just learnt would be my job, several therapies later, I thought I was destined to be a therapist and give Reiki healing via the treatments, and then spirit messages started to filter through as I gave treatments.

Thirteen years down the line, I thought I was destined to be a counselor, after four and a half years of training, and then for the following two years, spirit put me firmly back in the therapy saddle, with the messages finding their way through during the healing. Teaching, was the next step, classes in self-help, spiritual development, angels and masters classes and also another skills of regression, channeling and specific spiritual work which is part of my personal undertaking.

All filtering through, and now they move me onto a new path of reaching people though books, healing sound events, song, music, and guided mediation Cds.

Its Spirits show and you are simply a tool for light.

The counseling training I find is used with more dead clients than living, persuading those that are stuck on this plane that they shouldn't be here, and get them to move over to the next dimension.

The latest tool added to my spiritual tool bag has been sound healing which has led on to changing my vibratory level by using Sanskrit Manta, shamanic drumming, chant, a range of instruments and angelic toning, at this point planetary and high vibrational sounds are being channeled through, linked to the people who Rodger form London worked for and also the energy's which Sandy Stevens spoke of in the book 'The awakener' the second book of guidance given to me at the beginning of my journey, that in fact went straight over my head, recently I was given a chant to use from the same source,

I also now deliver the above sound formats in classes and workshops, and so the knowledge on to others to raise the individual's vibration, stimulates healing and I hope will help them reach their highest potential.

When I first gave messages, I found for me they came through mainly in picture form, in the beginning of my training, and I still see a lot of pictures. I am the kind of person who learns visually and I am more likely to remember a series of messages in visual form than in long verbal sentences. When I relay Spirit messages I may say, 'their giving you a…..' Words sometimes accompany the pictures, and now since I moved into the world of sound, songs are a part of messages. Giving the receiver of the message a song that becomes homework 'Go look up the words what they are telling you' I don't always remember what is channeled to me especially if I'm deep within the Spirit realms, so it's not uncommon for a person to say you said this or that, and it's not unusual for me to look back at them with a blank expression. I later learned to explain I can't always remember, because at the end of the day what was said was not a message for me, so unless I need to remember I won't. When the message receiving and giving part of my growth came into being, I was nervous at giving the messages that I received in case I was wrong or may be crazy. Logic was still taking every available opportunity to tell me it was imagination, and confidence telling me I was wrong. I have come across a number of people who want to be mediums and find their paths are blocked, they object strongly with statement like, 'Why can't I do it, I can hear them I know they are there, but they won't give me any more' I normally respond with explorative open questions like, 'What is the reason you want to be a medium' Often they want to talk to someone that has moved over that they knew, or have some other personal reason.

What they have to realise is these gifts are not given as personal toys, if you want to talk to Aunty Flo etc.

They will let you but it is on their terms not yours, if your heart genuinely wants to help others then the gift will be given.

If it's for self, it will be held back until you accept that it is a special gift worthy of commitment and devotion to the light.

In some cases it may not be beneficial or the right time, to have a particular ability, at this point in your spiritual growth, it may be you will learn something else first or you may work in another way.

Anyone who is going to relay Spirit messages also needs to be aware of boundaries; take care with what you say. You are responsible for the person's well-being that you are relaying the message to.

You need to think if the message you are about to give will cause upset, as some messages may have a detrimental effect on a person's life, you need to be self-aware and take responsibility for your actions. If you feel a message may cause someone distress, think about it, ask Spirit, tell them your concerns. If Spirit is insistent that you give the message, ask them if they can give the correct words. If it is going to be distressing, keep it to yourself.

You may find like me a message that sometimes a message must be relayed from Spirit will repeat, over and over in your head, it feels like your ears been chewed off and it won't go. On these occasions I say I have a message for you, and it won't go away and relay the message to the recipient.

If it is a difficult one I think about it and apply tact and diplomacy when passing it on, and try to soften the message. For example, I gave someone a treatment, I could see the cancer inside his body, and I couldn't leave it unsaid. How could I tell him? Logic having it's flash of prodding in my mind, saying what if you are wrong? So I explored another health issue and persuaded him to go to the doctor.

I will give you a few examples of instances when I felt it was not in the person's best interest to give a message.

Remember the when I spoke of new baby's souls remembering who they were until six weeks of age and how some new special souls do not forget, earlier in my book, this is the case I was referring to,

At a clairvoyant evening demonstration one good medium on stage sensitively said to the couple trying for a baby your child's very special it will be a crystal child, was she was instantly put down by another non -professional medium who then scalded her, 'Tell them as it is, your child going to be autistic' these kinds of comments are like a loaded gun and you can imagine the possible out comes from such a thoughtless and insensitive response.

Boundaries are important and vital. Not only that not all special children, are autistic, and autistic and other special souls have a pacific vibration required by the new vibrational fields which are now working on the planet, they are part of the future.

I met a young man who had always been a good sensible lad, he had been told he would be dead by the time he was twenty three, and so he went off the rails, deciding if he was going to die he would have a wild time first, he wasn't on a destructive path to begin with, the medium's message set him on one.

As I massaged a young dancer, her grandmother appeared bathed in pink light. She said, 'She will get through but her partner won't' I knew she had an audition for a scholarship at a dance academy coming up. Three days later I heard that she was given a scholarship and passed with flying colours; however her dancing partner did not get through. Had I have told her what might have happened, maybe she would not have danced so well, knowing she was going to make it, or perhaps she would have felt so bad for her friend she may have failed to get the scholarship.

I also met a man called Joe who had been told by a Medium that he had his tongue cut out for preaching the gospel in a past life. If that hadn't have been enough she told him that in another previous life he had preached Christianity and was stoned to death. The Medium used no tact or diplomacy, and simply blurted it out without thought or consideration for her client. This resulted in him becoming withdrawn, quiet and afraid to express his beliefs or opinions, for fear of repercussions upon him.

If you are relaying messages for Spirit, think before you speak find the balance and don't make the mistake that the Medium did with Joe.
Also just take note here - I have come across a number of cases where the Medium has been completely wrong in their interpretation of messages from Spirit.
Sometimes people want messages and there isn't any for them. I have seen Mediums slip into what we term as cold reading, because nothing has come through for the client, this is where the logical mind takes over looking for clues and phrases like 'I can see you have had a hard life' looking at hands that anyone can see have been aged by manual work, or a mark where the wedding ring had been, or displaying tired sad eyes. Body language gives a lot of implicit signs about a person, as a counselor and therapist this is the first thing I read when I greet a client, looking for the unspoken indicators and gestures. I have to get a sense of how my client is feeling physically and

emotionally, the way some one stands, walks, the way they
look in their face, the way they speak to me, hold their
shoulders, the way they sit in the chair. And that is before the
psychic kicks in.

We read so much from body language, quite naturally and you
don't need to be trained in reading it to know the basics.

This is a natural instinct of all human beings.

If you don't get a Spirit message for someone, be honest and
say, 'I'm not picking up anything, for you,' it is better to be
honest, than get a bad press. If spirit doesn't want to talk they
won't.

Please don't let the above cases put you of mediums there are
some excellent ones out there, and a high price tag doesn't
always mean they are the best.

In my experience medium-ship is often one of the first ability's
to come forward in a trainee.

As I worked with the therapies, over time I found each
treatment as different as the next. I felt spirit was showing me
there full range of power and how it was to be used.

Some people would receive powerful healing after one
treatment; in others it would trigger an awakening in them.

So they started their own growth and transformation.

I then found myself teaching others to help themselves, tips
and advice using therapeutic methods that could be applied by
them. Many clients became students and some members
became teachers, and work in a number of spiritual professions
themselves.

In the early days, when a person came to me for the first time,
I used to have no idea what they needed, I couldn't read body
language very well, however there higher self knows exactly
what they need.

So often a client would book something as simple as a
massage for stress or muscular problems, and may then find
they go away with a shopping list of herbs, vitamins and advice
from the spirit world to aid their healing. If they are, open
minded of course.

You eventually learn how to be tactful to non-believers giving
them the information that spirit wants you to give without them
realising a dead person told you.

Sometimes they suddenly tell you a story about for example
they saw Aunty Flo standing by their bed one night after she
had died. You have opened a little doorway and maybe that
night has left them wondering was it real? When their logic
says no, to them and their psyche says yes.

There is something in this, maybe logic may tell them well you
want to believe it, and so they will dismiss the signs from
spirit, at that point in time.

Then poor old psyche thinks I'll get my chance to prove it, just
you wait and see.

Sometimes you can explore an event like Aunty Flo visiting, if
they are of like mind and sometimes you can't, imagine telling
someone of closed mind that a dead person told you to say this.

Hark can't you hear the, black van coming in the distance
carrying the men in white coats.

You will learn who it's safe to tell over time, spirit always
finds a way to get their messages over to the recipient, as they
know the person they sent to you, better than you do.

They also have a bigger and better view of the situation than us
mortals on the earth plain.

Sometimes in a treatment it kicks a client's mind into realising
there is more to life than the material world, and spirit will give
whatever is required, to encourage them, whether it is healing,
a spirit message, energy clearing, or a development point,
perhaps there is an entity attachment.

❖

An entity may be a spirit who has not left the earth plan and lives within the aura of an individual; it can cause all kind of difficulties for them like, tiredness, irritability, to extremes of behavior changes that were not present before, they will cause some problems, and the entity needs removal. Some entities are of a lighter nature.

This however is not to be confused with mental health issues. Some people just need to talk about their experiences, just that once, they have never told anyone else for fear of ridicule, for example they thought they saw a man in the room, or a classic is glimpses of shadows passing by, written off to imagination, maybe a relative that came to them at night, they often feel a sense of relief, that these unexplained shadows and bumps in the night are real.

They don't need to call the men in white coats, with the shiny van, its ok they are not mad, and if they are, well hay, they can share their padded cell with yours truly;

The developing tool box

I had also discovered I had another line of work amongst my developing tool bag which seemed quite natural to me; it was something that I had been doing on a number of occasions in my life.

This was working with the dead, not on a message level originally but working with the dead who pass into your daily life, some call soul rescue. This is a way of helping the wandering dead find their way home. Or back to where they came from before they were born. Some lost souls may come in looking for someone else they have lost in the world of spirit, others can't rest for whatever reason they have, some don't want to move over they like it here.

There are those who are trapped here, and others may wish to work with you or even live with you for a while till they pass on.

This is just the tip of the iceberg there is much more to the world of Spirit, than we will ever know. As I grow I am amazed at how many kinds and types of dead there are, from numerous realms both light and dark. Yet if we look at the living we are also indeed very diverse beings, are we not?

As I mentioned some Spirits do like to lodge with me for a while, and I have lost count of how many I have had staying with me.

From ancients brought back from stone circles, to friendly relatives; small lost children but to name a few.

I have one such Spirit who often visits with us and is much loved, by all who become aware of his presence.

He was identified some years ago when Freya came for a treatment, she was a new client at the time, and a small man with a club foot heavily bandaged, came in on her second treatment it took me a while to be brave enough to say who he was.

She was well pleased about what happened.

'It's Uncle Jack' she responded excitedly, who turned out to be Freya's uncle, he makes us well aware of his love of chocolate. He liked to entertain the group attendees in the early classes, by causing us to fall into hysterical laughter. He appeared when the work needs an injection of humor to lighten the atmosphere.

There are Spirit children who stayed with me; some are lost looking for their mother's, or sad cases, where their short lives were very unpleasant, when they were in the material world. Often they had suffered abuse, cruelty, and death.

I couldn't help but feel over whelmed by sadness at these times. I find they use me like a substitute mother to feel safe and loved, until someone comes from the world of Spirit to take them home.

Mostly all any lost spirit needs, is love.

You will note I say home, for me I think of death as going home back to source from where everyone comes.

For the lost Spirits it is going home.

Several years later, at the time of writing this book, I now work with whatever department requires my services, as I find I have acquired a Spiritual tool bag that's getting to the stage it needs wheels on it. I feel as if I have more heads than *Wurzel Gummage.

*(Children's' television show in the late 70s about a scarecrow with different heads for different jobs)

You need to be aware, that when you come to this stage in your development and when you may be working with large numbers of people, you have to be careful they don't put you on a pedestal. If you like being on a pedestal, you need to take a good look at yourself. Then ask yourself, 'Is it ego creeping in' I remind them although it's me who appears to be giving the people what they need; they have to remember I am a conduit, Recall that empty cardboard toilet tube role again.

I always make it quite clear that I am just a channel, what the individual receives is not down to me, it is down to their higher self, and their higher consciousness, whatever they believe in, whether it be God, Allah, Goddesses or Fairies', or a universal life force, it doesn't matter.

All that is important is that they are helped along their life's path.

As I progressed through my growth I eventually came to realise that all the way through my development, I had rescued Spirits in one way or another. Unknowingly, it was a very natural ability. So when I started to visit the St Annes group, soul's gravitated to me for rescue. I had no problems or difficulties in stepping out of my world in to theirs and travelling with them, to help them find their way home.

I felt although I had been told that I had choices to make about the path, I had to take by Roger in London; I felt in my case I would follow my heart and simply go with the flow.

Trusting Spirit had worked out fine for me so far. So why should I doubt them to guide me to where I needed to be.

This meant things worked out quite well as I progressed, I trusted Spirit more and more and it was a natural transition to let them take the reins. This meant fewer arguments for me between logic and the psyche. Spirit knows which tools are needed for what job and brings to you, those who will benefit from your help.

There are times when you will feel disconnected from source. It feels as if all your abilities have left you. Don't worry its quite normal; in spiritual practice I call it 'The Wilderness', or 'Time out' this can happen for a number of reasons. The first one is to -

❖ Give you time to recharge after a period of growth or work, allowing the energy and vibrations you have experienced to filter through, and this in turn allows your personal vibration to become higher,

❖ It may occur if you become unstable mentally, life has many ups and downs we all experience times of instability, you need to be quite balanced when working within the world of Spirit, or the men in white coats will come.

❖ If you prefer spending too much time in the world of Spirit and not enough in the material world, which I hold my hand up to, 'Yes my lord, I'm guilty as charged' It might be withdrawn until you reach balance again between the material and spiritual worlds.

❖ If you get too big for your boots for example, and view the gifts or abilities as if saying 'Look at me aren't I powerful' Then sooner or later Spirit will kick you in the ass, or to put it politely pull the plug. If that is the case they may simply take your abilities away to teach you a lesson, sometimes permanent or temporarily. Or It may be given back in small bits and bobs or only when needed.

❖ If you become too ill to work and need to heal yourself

On the whole, most spiritually minded people work from the heart and after a flurry of Spiritual or energy activity where you have been working very hard for the world of spirit, whichever energy type you are working with you will find things may become very quiet. At these times you find yourself wondering if they will talk to you ever again, or if you will feel or see the energy or Spirit again.

Once more, rest assured, when you have filtered the energy and experience's through you, you will start to feel stronger spirit energy's, and in turn be able to work at a higher level, we all need rest from this work it's like any other job, you will need a holiday or a few days off.

Spirituality and energy work in cycles; for example the Rune Stones would say ice, thaw, and spring, birth, growth, fruition, death, then back to the ice stage again. You will soon notice the cycles in life, not just in spiritual life but also life in generally.

In the early stages it may seem more like you spend more time switched off than on. You're champing at the bit and rearing to go, you have had a taste of what can be and you miss it, when it's not there.

Please try to be patient, at this stage see yourself as a snowdrop lying beneath the snow waiting to pop your head up as the snow melts away. For me this ice stage is a quiet time, little spiritual activity, no one booking treatments, time out to work with life chores or hobbies.

I have learnt to accept this and focus on whatever else needs doing in my everyday life whether its washing the curtains, catching up on paper work, or just using the time to get things done, it will be back soon enough, be patient.

Then there is the thaw stage as it sets in, I would start with Astral Projection and vivid dreams, my head feels a little fuddled, and I feel unearthed and have to concentrate on grounding myself as the energy flow increases.

Then a calmness and a growth stage, as the process starts all over again. People call for treatments, and spiritual events increase, new knowledge is gained and my mind becomes very

clear, then it reaches a peak, before it settles down again
and I am given time out to recharge, once again.
When you have timeout, take the opportunity to catch up with
whatever you need to do.
You may also find yourself, doing quite the opposite not
allowing time for your spiritual development. You may be
working so much before you know it feels like it has all passed
you by,
Remember no moment or few minutes are lost in spiritual
growth, even five minutes of Mantra, or a quick energy
channeling exercise, are so important for your development
and linking up with spirit.
A little is better than none at all.
In the earlier days, I wanted to have a spiritual life so badly but
there never seemed to be time, at one stage I found myself
working as a therapist, cleaner, P/A and in a fish shop, to make
ends meet for my family.
Needless to say my health condition that I had been fighting
took a turn for the worse.
Another comparison I can give you is when I was cleaning
twelve houses a week, until a man brought me to a swift bump
back to earth.
He was a Buddhist Priest I had met at the Nottingham group in
St Annes. He repeatedly tapped me on the head saying in his
Broken English 'Busy, busy, busy you're going nowhere you?'
His words ringing in my mind, I didn't like what he said it
made me feel cross and frustrated at the time. However, he was
absolutely right.
You may find you are doing the following like I did.
You may be working, running a home, looking after your
husband/partner and children, tending animals family, friends,
there are the house repairs the garden, little Johnnie's football,
Melissa's tennis, your work out, if you have time.

All the issues that come within life's rich tapestry and like I did, you may find yourself saying, 'Where am I going to find the time' your too tired at the end of the day to even think about anything spiritual or connecting to an energy source.

I have been there, so I do understand how hard it can be. I'm well aware of the difficulties you might face.

Try taking one step at a time, all my growth and development still carried on regardless of my work load, if you hunger for it enough it will happen,

Like a mouse with a big piece of cheese nibble away and you will get there, one thing to remember is

IT IS DOABLE!

You will find your own way around it, I am sure.

So there is no time like the present!

'How about starting tonight? Or right now'

Here is a simple way to start bringing energy in and also relaxation into your life.

It will help you to grow and the energy you bring in will in turn create more energy, and help you to channel more and more over time.

Simple Starting Exercises

This exercise brings in energy in the form of colour therapy; try to get into the habit and if you can keep notes of your experiences, that too will be an advantage to your personal development.

Begin with the first step. Maybe start this when you go bed at the end of the day

- Breath in a few relaxed breaths

- Place your hands on yourself wherever feels comfortable.
- Then imagine a colour.
- Now imagine this colour filtering through your body from the top of your head to the tips of your toes.
- As it leaves your toes visualize the colour that leaves your feet has turned into grey smoke. This smoke carrying away all the stress and strains of the days, and any aches and pains.
- Now imagine yourself filling up with another colour, a soothing healing colour.
- Imagine it flowing through you and around you, healing, strengthening, revitalizing, soothing, calming.

Don't worry if you fall asleep before you finish this exercise. You can also break it down into bite size pieces. For example:- Bring the colours in one night. When you have got the hang of that, see the smoke leaving your feet the next night, then maybe the following night visualize yourself filling up with the final colour.

You will soon master the skill of visualization and find you can carry out the whole process quite easily in a matter of a few minutes.

So you see! You have made a start at bringing energy into your life; it's as easy as that.

If you continue with a range of small exercise like this you will, be amazed at how much you as an individual have grown in a year. That is why I suggest writing a few notes as a reminder, Even if it's just now and again. You can also adapt the above exercise when you need a few moments of calm, courage or to recharge,

- ❖ Think about what you want, i.e., healing, strength, calm and balance etc.

- ❖ Think of a colour, the first one to pop in your mind. You instinctively know what colour you need to heal at that time, so trust in the process
- ❖ Focus on the colour,
- ❖ Take it all the way through you top of the head to the tip of the toes,
- ❖ Visualize it flowing all around you like a cloud ,
- ❖ See all the feelings, thoughts pain, etc anything that is negative leave your feet as a grey smoke.
- ❖ Ask the Spirit of light to take the negative away, you can ask anything you believe in that is of light from Angels, Fairies etc. It's your visualization and your choices to make.

Breaking the exercise into smaller pieces will make it easier, if like me you struggle to retain what you have read.
Like I said, 'A small mouse with a big piece of cheese' it's already smaller than when you started.
Another starting point you can also explore is the phrase,
When we sometimes say, 'The thought is the deed' so you could try asking the Universal Light to heal you while you rest, or ask them to help you solve your problems, find a solution and to cope with life's ups and downs, in REM sleep we are more susceptible to the suggestions form the higher source.

Instead of lying there worrying you can empower yourself, you don't have to sit passively by when life kicks you in the bum. You could try this, a simple Mantra to calm your mind, you know when thoughts go around and around like a hamster on a wheel.
'Om hum om hum' it has multi uses, it connects you to universal energy source, and Hum in its self is good for calming the mind, it dispels illusions and brings clarity to the thought process, and also has a protective element.

Simply chant in your head, or out aloud if you are alone,
and if you can't sleep, it has vibrational frequencies that also
the release of chemicals in the brain

Remember we have to ask Spirit for help, the reason being we
are mortals operating by freewill, the spiritual world can't
assist us if we don't ask them to, because that may be classed
as interfering in our freewill. But rest assured, when you do
ask, they will help you in a way that is for your highest good. It
may not be quite as you would have planned it.

You can extend all these using the simple practice of
visualization, in so many ways, using different colours,
energies, vibrations. You can play relaxation tapes, soft healing
music. Maybe taking your Reiki One, attunement or find some
other form of energy source; that you can incorporate into your
life.

The range is vast and there will be something out there that fits
with your life style and feelings.

The Need to Earth

You will need to learn another important exercise, when you
start using energy, it is called `Earthing', or grounding
yourself, you will need to do this with whatever form of energy
you are using, or you will become unsteady.

After working with energy whether in the form of colour or for
example spirit, reiki etc learn to earth, it can also be used
generally when you feel shaky or unstable in any way.

You will have noticed I have mention Earthing before, when I
recounted the situation I found myself in when I was absorbing
other people's negative emotions, before I bought the Selfic
Disk from the Damanher. It is quite simple to do, and also
essential, you can start by visualising.

- Red roots coming from your pelvis down your legs and out of your feet,
- See them growing down deep into the earth,
- As you see your roots grow they become stronger and thicker, keeping you well balanced, strong and stable.
- You can visualize your roots tying themselves to a rock or a crystal, in the ground, or burying them in the soil.
- Perhaps you prefer to visualise yourself standing on a beach, your feet on the wet sand, sinking slightly, and the sea lapping over you as the soft caressing surf ripples around your ankles.
- A quick and practical method is to rinse your wrists under a cold tap, this will also earth you. This method is one I use in between treating clients or when group healing.
- Give yourself time to re-adjust, before you continue with whatever you are doing

Just as a matter of interest here are a couple of examples of clients not being earthed after having therapy treatments although they were not working with energy at a conscious level the higher consciousness allowed energy to flow through them during their therapy.

A colleague of mine asked her client to take a few minutes, have a cup of tea and earth before, he left. He refused saying, 'He was fine' He drove out of the driveway straight into a wall across the street.

Another example was when a client of mine refused to earth dismissing it as rubbish. He had been a traffic police man for thirty years and knew the area very well. He rang me a week later, 'You know that earth thing you told me about?' He said 'Earthing', came my reply feeling a little smile cross my face, I knew what he was going to say, 'Well you were right I got lost twice between your house and the A1' he said in disbelief and an awareness that there was some truth in what I said.

The A1 was barely two minute drive from my home at that time.

There are other exercises, and more in-depth lessons in my book 'Release Your Phoenix'.

So enjoy the adventure and don't put too much pressure on yourself, take it a step at a time and enjoy and trust the growth process. See the above exercise as your first keys to unlock new doors.

I have just at this point been told to tell you,

'You can use energy in everyday life, it is available to everyone, no exceptions it transcends religion, and can be proved within the world of quantum physics, and the spiritual part is an added extra. It's up to you whether you believe or not. You can still use energy.

Even if you don't believe in the spiritual part.

Another Door, and a New Set of Keys.

It was 2001, and I was now at the stage of my growth, where I messages were a regular occurrence verbally and in detailed picture form. However I was still very nervous about giving messages, and most of the time I didn't relay the messages. My search for my own kind, a never ending and lonely quest, I was blessed and grateful for the Nottingham group, although I felt inside I didn't quite fit, although everyone was so kind and supportive.

I was still taking the opportunities to visit mind, body and spirit fairs, searching for my own kind hoping to find some mortal guide, I had resigned myself to the fact that Roger from London would not be contacting me and as usual I felt very alone.

One day while visiting a fair, in Newark, I wandered around, as usual nothing really connecting with me and feeling disappointed. I then saw a friend of Mary's who was my first Reiki Master she had planted the seed in me in 1998, now I was a small sapling, in need of feeding.

Mary's friends name is Julie, I stood for a while talking to her, my hands began to take on the familiar tingling feeling as the Reiki energy began to flow.

I knew that it was for Julie, but being a Reiki One student and Julie a Reiki Master I was not sure what to say to her, Julie then broke the ice.

'I feel you are here to give me something' she said.

I told her about the Reiki in my hands and she encouraged me to go and stand with her behind her stand, I proceeded to put my hands on her shoulders, the energy flooded in, and I felt somewhat humble. Within minutes I was being shown pictures by spirit, they were bright and clear like the dreams about the man in black. But this time they were small snapshots of pictures. As if a camera lens had zoomed in on the object, they repeated themselves over and over, with such clarity. However my tongue was firmly stuck in my mouth and the familiar feeling of words not coming out of my mouth, just like the time when I went to deliver my first spirit message in Manchester to the man in black.

Julie knew instinctively that I was picking something up and encouraged me to say what I was seeing. I relayed the visual message to her, it related to a family matter. Julie had been dealing with, it did bring comfort.

It was also verification for me that the men with the black van and the half a pound of jelly babies could in fact go home. I wasn't crazy. I really, wasn't crazy.

A couple of years later Julie and I became close friends and worked often with each other we had many beautiful spiritual experiences, helping me to grow from a small sapling into a small tree.

I then went on to take my Reiki two with Julie; this seemed to tie up some emotional loose ends, and letting go of some of the things in my life that I held on to.

I had no intention of ever taking a Reiki Master's degree. I was happy where I was.

Then one day she looked at me and said, 'I'm being told to give you your Reiki Masters.'

'I can't afford it' I replied. I was somewhat surprised it had never entered my head, that I would attain a higher level of Reiki. I would have never considered myself worthy.

She smiled, 'That is ok, I'm being told to give you it and you will pay me back one day'

And so I took my masters and a year later my circumstances changed suddenly: relationship number four ended, I sold the house and paid Julie the money I owed her as she said I would.

Working with Julie gave me a great deal of confidence and helped my growth and development progress, and for a while I had a mortal guide and so many wonderful experiences.

Many of which bring tears to my eyes as I recall them.
However, they are stories for another time.

The Nottingham group had given me confidence and protection during my growth and transformation; we shared love and laughter with this world and the next,
We would always start the group with a prayer followed by meditation. I have never been able to empty my mind as some books instruct you to do, when it comes to mediations, there's too much going on in my head for that. I call it Hamster in a wheel others say monkey mind. I have found this to be quite common event.
Some people are put off by the word meditation, and afraid to try because their minds are whizzing all over the place.
Making one's mind blank or an empty space and keeping it that way, is a very difficult to do, remember it is not necessary to blank your mind, in order to mediate so you need not miss out.
When you are of a more advanced level you will find it easier to clear and blank your mind.
In the early days, I would relax and found I slipped into a trance like state of mind. I would go with spirit on a journey; sometimes the journey would be one that helped me solve a problem for a spirit, myself or someone else. It's like a type of Spiritual Counseling.
Although I did not know that a few years down the line I would in fact become a counselor.

One example I recall, when I needed help for a personal issue.

I took a few controlled breaths, relaxed, and entered into an altered state of awareness. I was still having moments of trouble and doubts about my sanity which bit me in the bum at any time it chose.

A spirit came to me and taking me by the hand we walked between fluffy clouds and blue sky. As I looked back a dark shadow was following me, I felt safe with the Spirit who walked with me, feeling a tremendous amount of love.

Although I knew I was safe and loved, I also knew I had to get rid of the shadow that followed me. At this point I saw a slit like opening within the cloud; I grabbed the shadow, as if grabbing someone by the scruff of the neck and bungling it into the gap. I physically felt myself pushing and shoving and forced it though the gap, it struggled against me determined not to go. I fought with all my might to push it in.

Then in my mind I created a zip on the opening and as I stuffed it in a little at a time and zipped up the opening a little further following each push, I succeeded in pushing more of the shadow through.

I could hear the leader of the group calling us back from our meditation, I knew I couldn't leave until I had completed my task; so I carried on bungling the shadow in to the gap and zipping it up until I had it well and truly secured.

It was explained to me by the spirit that the shadow represented doubt, lack of trust, fear. I was loved and protected by my Spirit guides, and in my meditative state, I had vanquished my fears and the things that were holding my development back at that time of my growth. Once the shadow had gone this meant I could move forward.

Eventually the Nottingham group folded, it had ran its course; the chicks had flown the nest, they had been given the keys needed and flown on to new adventures

I missed the companionship of like-minded people, and I so longed for a group to be with.

In 2002 I had attempted to start my own group, and held one which had quite an effect on the attendees; however it was destined not to come in to fruition, until I moved home to Mansfield in 2005.

Within two weeks of moving to my new home in among a mishmash of missing floor boards, half built walls and dangling electric wires, paint pots and boxes piled high containing my worldly goods, the new group began to form.

Being in new home, there was so much to do, and starting a gathering of like minds was very much down the bottom of the to do list, I'm the sort of person who can't work or study or write if the area around me untidy, my head will not function or settle.

As I stood up a ladder painting the walls, I received a phone call from Freya; she stated a friend of hers was in serious trouble. In fact it was one of the friends, she had planned to bring to see me, prior to me moving to Mansfield some time ago, it did not happen for one reason or another.

Her friend was having problems with negative spirits who had come to collect a debt.

Little did I know that this phone call was the beginning of a new group, a gathering of like minds.

I had attempted to make happen before unsuccessfully, and now without my realising, the egg of the phoenix lay in the bottom of the nest.

This time it was spirits choice of time scale and when spirit says, 'The time is now' no amount of excuses will make a difference. And a house in disarray was at the bottom of their list.

So the new group, started with two strangers who came for help, via Freya's telephone call.

One was later to become my fiancé. I would have met him some years previous, had the meeting taken place as we had agreed when I lived at Tuxford. Freya had met them some time before and she had already asked to bring them to see me, as I stated above, and I had agreed, however the lady who was now to come to me in Mansfield, and so we never met until three weeks after I moved into my new home, at the early part of September 2005.

Before the Nottingham group ended, a group member, gave me a message from the world of spirit, she said
'You will not find what you are looking for with this group, there is a symbol on a book, you will recognise it, when you see it......This is what you are'

Friends in Words

So the answer to what I was would be on a book, what would
the symbol be? What book? Where would I find it?
I wondered, there where so many books, so many pictures and
symbol's, nevertheless this symbol would tell me what I was,
Spirit had told me I was a star child and this made sense giving
backing to all the thoughts and deeper feelings I had as a child,
although they didn't tell me what a star child was and what I
was supposed to do with all these ability's or gifts of which
were now increasing, my grandmother said a gift came with the
name Zillah, but which gift.
What was this mysterious symbol? Whatever it was, would
answer the big question, well one of them anyway!
It was no great surprise that it was to be a book to solve one of
my many questions, 'What am I?'
Books have always played an important part in my
development with spirit, in the early development days; I found
it worked like this;
I would have a spiritual experience, and then after I had been
through the mill and worked out what had happened to me, it
would be confirmed in a book some weeks later.
My main supporting book at the time was Betty Shine's 'My
Life as a Medium'. I felt I was a mini Betty Shine, I had no
idea what I was to become, and I never expected to be what I
am now.
Events would happen in my life, and then if I was having
difficulties understanding what was happening to me, I would
sit with the book and concentrate on what I wanted to know,
I would open it randomly and sure enough most of the time the
answer I needed would be there, then again on some occasions
I had to learn the hard way and sometimes it was like riddles
left as clues, on a mystery weekend or an Easter egg hunt.

Many books can be used like this and I know other faiths
do this with books like, The Bible or God calling books, etc.
It could be any Spiritual book that you feel connected with
often it will give you guidance, or confirmation.
It could be viewed as an oracle such as the rune stones or tarot
cards. There are many types to choose from.
Find what resonates with you and work with it !

I had so many experiences with Betty Shine's book,
'My life as Medium'.
One occasion before leaving the farm in 1998, I had been
reading the book early one Saturday morning; I found I had
dosed off, suddenly I woke up to the sensation and feeling of
water running in my hands. I opened my eyes suddenly,
thinking I would see water, and my nightdress would be wet, it
was not. Strangely the book also felt wet, but was not, I
thought maybe my hands were sweaty but they were not

On another occasion when I was in a confused state at the time
when I had a foot in each world, I was feeling very upset and
lonely, I sat on the edge of my bed, not knowing what to do
with myself, a bright light suddenly appeared on the spine of
the book that sat on my bookshelf, the room was gloomy, it
was a dull and rainy day, there was no sunlight shining in or
lamp lit, just the edge of the that book lit up, no other.
It looked as if someone had shone a torch beam directly on it.

The same book confirmed my findings, when I experienced my
first visual sighting of a Spirit possession.
This is what happened.
I found myself having to collect a friend in the early hours of
the morning to take him home as he had missed his lift, had no

money left and rang me for help. He was going through a
bad patch and he was worse the ware with alcohol, and not in
control of his faculties. I went to his rescue, and panicked when
I found he was not by the river as he had said, I feared the
worse. I eventually found him, at one point I turned to look at
him, looking directly into his eyes, as I spoke, a chill filtered
through me like jack frosts fingers, the eyes that stared back
were not my friends green eyes.
In their place, eyes as dark and cold as black glass, they glinted
and seemed emotionless, like those of a shark.
I was unnerved to say the least and chanted the only real
protection that I knew at the time, the Lord's Prayer, which I
chanted all the way back home.

I lay in bed tired but unable to sleep, the memory of the nights
event filtered through my mind, until, the night seemed to
disappear quickly and dawn broke, the suns morning rays,
breaking tenderly over the fields, I knew a hard day's work of
cleaning houses lay just ahead. I felt so tired, and questioned
what I had seen.
The day came and I ran on adrenalin as usual, house to house
counting the hours left from every job complete, I felt very odd
for the most part of the day and put it down to the lack of sleep.
The children were away that evening, and I sat reading, and
writing college course work, taking some quiet time to myself,
and promising myself an early night in the safety of
'Highfields' wrapping me in its protective walls, I sat snuggled
in the warmth and safety of my bed, and tried to catch a couple
of hours of sleep.
I had had a craving for alcohol, about seven o'clock, that
evening and I ignored it, a sensation I hadn't felt for a very
long time, the craving became so bad that by nine o'clock, I
found myself getting dressed and getting into the car, driving
three miles, to the shop to purchase a bottle of vodka, not even

my tipple. Several glasses later I felt sober, which was the second unusual event, as you know I'm cheap to run, as half a pint of larger is enough to send me, well wobbly.

The sudden feeling of a light bulb moment hit, as realisation dawned yet again on this path of learning. I came to recognise that this was not my feelings but in fact someone else's feelings and emotions.

The old grey matter began to put two and two together and I worked out that I had picked up some sort of attachment from my friend that was not mine. I didn't really know what to do, this was a new lesson. I had no one to ask, for clarification.

So once more I looked at my book shelf choosing the one I was drawn to. I then ran a bath, the Betty Shine book 'My Life as a Medium 'went with me;

I felt very close to Betty although we never met until two years later after her death, which was a magical moment I will always treasure.

I lay in the bath and relaxed slipping down into the bubbles holding the book up high so the suds didn't touch it.

I allowed the book to open where ever it wished. Sure enough its pages flicked by my slightly damp fingers, opened at a section in a chapter explaining how we could take on other people's habits, from the spirit world when they attached themselves to our auras.

It all fell into place and even though my brain was soaked in vodka, I felt sober and my mind felt quite clear, I had been with my friend in the early hours of that morning, and it was a spirit of negative energy's that had attached itself to him on his night out in town, and in my inexperience state it had quite easily attached itself to me, by the way of my auric field, placing its feelings, and needs upon me.

As I grew some years later I was able to see the Spirits that had attached themselves to other people auras, unfortunately at the time they were the kind of entities that fed off a host and they were of a darker nature. All I could do at that phase was to surround the person involved with an energy field of light to make the spirit step away. I did not know how to remove them or send them home, and quite often a host will let a spirit re-attach for a number of reasons often not even being aware it had taken place.

Hidden from me in 1999 was a whole new adventure regarding spirit attachment. I wasn't to know that eight years later within my work, I would be able to collect them, find, trap and remove them.
My guides working hard to make sure they would leave their host with or without permission, and where they are released isn't always pleasant.
I have mentioned auras throughout my book. You may already know what an aura is.
If you don't, don't worry I have explained at length about auras later in this book and also how to protect you from such occurrences like the one above, although negative spirits on most part, need a negative vibrational environment in which to thrive, drugs, alcohol, anger, and depression are ideal situation's for the negative forms to attach themselves to a host.

For now here is just a basic explanation regarding auras, so it is a little clearer.
The aura is an electromagnetic energy field which surrounds living things, the halo you see on religious figures is the aura, however we all have one not just holy or religious people.
The first layer of the aura is nearest the body, and so it has particles in it, like dust and skin this is why it is the easiest part of the aura to see. It has several layers of different colours and reflects mental, physical and spiritual health, it also has sound vibrations that can be measured in hz

The symbol

My life has changed so much, and I have only told you some of the events that led me to the here and now.

Amongst this book, words are coming together for other books. At one point, I was holding down four part-time jobs, doing groups and workshops and so you see as I said, 'It is do able.' And so I take you forwards to late 2000 and the mystery of the symbol.

Remember the member of the healing group who told me I wouldn't find what I was looking for with them, she said I would find a book with a symbol on and that would show me what I was.

She was right about the symbol; what I didn't realise is I had in fact already been shown it, and I didn't understand its significance, it was also to appear via my friend Sue, who had traveled with me to G-Mex in Manchester, when I delivered my message to the man in black.

Love had entered her life and she had met her handsome prince and was in the process of selling her house. She offered me a box of items that she no longer wanted, and in the box was a print by Andrew Forest. I was very drawn this beautiful print and as I looked at the very bottom, there resting between two dragon like creatures, was a symbol which I immediately felt drawn to.

The symbol on the picture was the tree of life as some call it, it is also the labyrinth. I didn't put the information together at the time; I just felt a connection to the symbol. I had not realised that I had already been through a labyrinth with the vision created by the Selfic disk which I bought from the Damnhur. I just simply fell in love with the artist's detailed work and took the picture home with me; giving it pride of place in my own little sanctuary, 'Highfields'.

At this part of my development symbols were generally playing an important role in my life, I didn't know what they were for or their significance. I felt spirit place them on my forehead, from time to time, and they would change periodically. I could also see what colour and shape they were. I didn't understand their meanings or why I had them placed on my head by Spirit. They could be anything from circles, diamonds, stars or geometry shapes that were not familiar to me at the time.

My search for others like myself was a never ending quest, saving any article I came across which mentioned anything spiritual. I notice that spiritual story's only seemed to appear in newspapers, of a more gritty nature. In those days, I felt that they sensationalized the topic, but in reality they were ridiculing it. I thought there must be some newspapers somewhere that looked at it in a more serious vain and viewed it with a more scientific point of view; after all man thought the world was square at one time.

One of the things I had found via the Kindred Spirit magazine was a book company who specialized in a range of mind body and spirit books, most of them were well above my understanding at this stage. However that didn't quell my excitement one bit, it was like a chocoholic being given the biggest Easter egg they could only dream about, and the Easter bunny would have been glad he didn't have to carry it.

I indulged myself and spent a small fortune on books, I read so many and it has resulted in quite a collection, some of the books that I read I didn't really understand what they were talking about.

Although re-reading them a few years later when you have grown you often understand them better, so save them don't give them away just yet.

I sat with the magazine making my choice of books for that month even though I knew I should be saving my money for

other things it always seemed to pan out and I got the ones
I wanted. I looked through the booklet making lists of ones I
defiantly wanted, then maybes and possible in my choices,
Unexpectedly a symbol jumped out at me from the pages.
It was like someone slapping me around the head with a wet
fish; it was so sudden and surprising. I recognised it as the
same symbol that was on the Andrew Forest print, that Sue had
given me a few weeks earlier.
The book was called the 'Soul Rescuers', by Terry and Natalia
O' Sullivan.
I ordered the book and my eager little hands couldn't wait for it
to arrive. When it did come, I felt a connection with the book
before I even opened it.
It has a vibrant purple book cover with a silver labyrinth; I ran
my fingers over the symbol.
This symbol was the key to what I was.
I read the book from cover to cover more than once, there were
so many comparisons, this coupled with the events I had been
experiencing over the last four years, created a clear
understanding to what had been happening, and was still
happening in my life,
I understood it completely.
I had no psychic or logic questioning or arguing, and a
temporary peace and calm filled my heart and mind.
If a book could have been written for me personally, at that
time of my growth then that was the one.
At last I knew what I was, 'A Soul Rescuer'.

This is where my journey really took on a new life of its own,
Betty Shine's books had been like a spiritual mother to me in
the early days from 1997, and a number of her books supported
my growth, even now I send her love and light and I will never

forget her support guidance at the time of my first faltering steps, and her rare fleeting visits after her death. I send out my heartfelt thanks, and I hope my books will help others as Bettys helped me.

I still have an original signed copy of 'My Life as a Medium' as well as later books, and like all good books it doesn't matter how big a tree you grow into, it is still a positive thing to still draw on them from time to time and remember your roots..

I could see my spiritual tool bag growing larger too, and thanks to the books written by others, I understood the process of my growth, and development a little clearer.

When I looked back at this point to get a sense of how far I had come and also reading the old diaries, acts as a reminder of so many lessons.

It had all started with a series of dreams in 1996, then meeting Mary and the start of training to be a therapist in 1997, Mary introduced me to a source of energy Reiki. Spirit had shown me how it could be used, and the other energies, along with abilities to receive and give spirit messages; I could feel energy and see it in some of its forms. As my ability to use energy grew, I began to see colours, and auras.

Through more lessons spirit taught me to use protection, and draw negative spirits out of people's auras.

Casting a penny in the wishing well at lock ness, found me, within reach of the Nottingham group in 1999 to 2000, due to the fact I had no confidence in my own ability's to carry out reflexology, I then met, Brenda, Anne and Wendy.

The group had given me the love and safety in which to grow. I was at this stage a daisy waiting to open up, I hadn't yet met Julie my final reiki master and in a way I still felt a bit lost and alone, feeling I was different, I was still not sure where I belonged or who I belonged with.

The first tentative step to becoming what I was, with my moving to Highfields in 1998 there it felt that spirit was enough for me, I needed no more, and yet in my mind I still yearned for a mortal to walk with me and guide me, reassuring me I didn't need to call the nice men in the white jackets with the big black van to come and collect me.

A new direction was now forming; The soul rescue book had given me a key to open a door of new understanding.

However I was still very lonely searching for my own kind was a constant quest.

The World of the Soul Rescuer

It is now 2013/14 and my world is not like any other I could
have ever imagined all those lessons and experiences,
loneliness, fear and joy came in the right order and at the right
time. Although at the time of the events, none of it made much
sense. Now it makes perfect sense and as I grow I wait with
anticipation wondering where my journey will take me next.
Who will I meet, and where will it end.
And so I will try to give you a little insight into my world when
I was working as a Soul Rescuer in 1999 to 2008.
Although now I work in many other dimensions and areas of
spirituality, I didn't know existed in the early years, this is part
of my growth and journey, and yours will follow its own
unique path.
In 2000 I was named as a walker between worlds spirit gave
me the title and like the name star child it shed light on my
understanding of what I was and my purpose.
What you are named does not really matter, it is how well you
perform your tasks that count, like attaining the title of Reiki
master, you are not a true master until you have earned it, and
that comes from the hearts domain.
In December 2012, I was presented by spirit with the title of
shadow-walker, for another reason I have at this stage, in this
my first book, removed anything of a darker nature, I do not
want to alarm or unnerve you at this phase of your
development. The worlds I walk within are parts of my path of
service. Your paths or worlds may be very different to mine.

The first thing I can say from a Soul Rescuer's, point of view,
is it felt totally natural to me too step from one world in to the
other, I don't find it difficult in any way, and I'm humbled
and blessed to be allowed to work in this field with the world
of Spirit.

I don't need to send myself into deep meditations, or focus on creating altered states of awareness. I simply close my eyes connect to source and Spirit has me there.

At first, within the safety of the Nottingham group, lost Spirits came to me. The pictures appeared and disappeared, away we went to wherever I was needed, then I was brought back, the lost spirits went home, job done. Quite simple, really; I'm always aware that it is not me, who does this, I am just a channel.

That cardboard toilet tube again !

I have total trust in the powers that work through me.

My gift is still growing and I can now be in this world and the world of Spirit at the same time. My work now is more diverse in this field than I could ever have anticipated. However, journeying it is still the one gift I feel more at ease with.

What is a soul rescuer?

Well they are many mediums who also rescue souls, in all kinds of ways, never the less the way I and my kind work is different and it has a blend of angelic and shamanic leanings. We live our lives like everyone else, with the exception that we can move between the physical world and the spiritual world plus the other realms with great ease.

For the Soul Rescuer or walker moving between worlds they need to remain balanced and connected, they need to live in this world, but be not of it. Spirit is in control of the channel, and they can be called upon at any time and any place to work as required. There aren't set times to connect, and work is not to a schedule. It is simply that their gifts are need when the universal light says so.

Their faith must be unwavering, and they put the universal force needs before their own needs, they are also willing to make sacrifices in their personal life, often some of these sacrifices are painful and can involve leaving those they love behind. They also need to be in control of their ego, and be committed to world service. Sometimes they are truly misunderstood by colleagues or friends

It is a lonely path which they follow as they often feel there isn't anyone who really understands their feelings surrounding the kind of work they do. Much of what they know and do, they have to keep to themselves because, it sounds completely insane, and also there is the need to protect others.

They do still have the choice to say no, and leave this path, if they so wish, they are never forced to work for spirit; they operate by free will just like every other spiritual worker. Soul rescuers made a commitment and chose to walk this path long ago and to work in this specific way.

They like many people working for spirit, they are connected by a umbilical type cord which connects them between the worlds, and all its dimensions, it is said there are one hundred and eight threads to the cord, which connects our physical and subtle energy, within this there are seventy two thousand energy channels, and just as a matter of interest there are seventy two thousands nerve endings in your feet.

The Soul Rescuer's belief in their faith is steadfast and solid and doubts must not be allowed to creep in at any time.

If there were any kind of doubt in their belief in spirit, they would be vulnerable to the negative energy's which would undoubtedly find its way in.

For me personally I say, 'love is my shield and my faith is my sword'. I have no doubts about the light Spirits that guide and protect me, I never doubt them and I do not believe they will ever give me a task that is above my capabilities. Some tasks may be harder than others and I might struggle but that is part of learning and growing.

There are so many kinds of tasks and jobs that need doing, like entities that rise up from the lower astral realms that need dealing with, they do their best to undermine and confuse.

They are cleaver, devious and hide in the strangest places;
they will try to trick you and try to stop your growth.
It is also not a job for the faint hearted. It can be very
unnerving even for a professional Soul Rescuer.

A good thing to remember for any person working in the world
of spirit is to be, 'Aware of your limitations' you should not be
stubborn or afraid to ask for the assistance from others when
needed.
Also choose carefully who you take with you and on what job.
Don't take any one who isn't skilled enough to deal with your
situation or you may put yourself and them in danger.
When it is a Soul Rescue session that is what I call normal, for
example, when someone is lost or looking for someone, I am
aware of what is happening around me, but also what is
happening in the Spirit world too. I would interact with you in
a vague sort of way.
There are times when I am not here and out of my body in an
altered state of awareness this is when I am not attentive to
what is happening in the physical world, and this is a time
when ideally, you should have a colleague to watch over you.
Soul rescuers do not work alone, we are like a cog in the
wheels of an old grandfather clock, and we are attached to
many guides, guardian spirits and spirit's helpers of varying
types so that we are able to perform our task.
Think of a Soul Rescuer as 'The lantern that attracts the moths'
and in some cases moths get caught or burnt.
I will tell you some story's about some of my early soul rescue
experiences later and my book 'The Phoenix in the Shadows',
explains about the darker aspects of the work with negative
Spirits.

Well you may well wonder what's it like when you are in the
world of Spirit, if you haven't yet experienced it. I can only

give you a small comparison and a little insight into what I feel and know, from my perspective.

If you were blind and in a room alone you would be aware of someone entering the room, perhaps you could sense them standing near you, or smell a change in the air. Even if you did not hear them enter; your other senses are more finely tuned to make up for the lack of sight

It can also feel like that dream state where you question, am I awake or asleep, or am I dreaming.

A classic example, you physically need the bathroom, and your bodies not woken up, in your dream state you're looking for a toilet, sounds familiar?

When I first started to work within the realm of Spirit, I sensed a Spirit presence by the changes in the energies around me.

My heart rate rising tells me some one is coming close.

Communication is by telepathy, there are normally no language barriers. Sometimes however, it is difficult to hear what they are saying if the spirit communicating hasn't got the hang of using the energies to make themselves heard.

Also recently an ancient language came through which made my tongue physically painful as it sounded so guttural.

Spirit can be seen in many different ways, sometimes they are whole beings, as solid as you or I. Sometimes they are only partly visible, a side of a person or half a body, just arms, shadows, or silhouettes. They can be seen as light energy taking on many other forms such as a mist, smoke, coloured lights, the feeling of heat or cold.

These can make the hairs stand up on your body, or the feelings like a breeze or a strong draft near you, a gentle touch like a cob-web glancing across your face.

Some Spirits are well able to use electric, telephones and move objects; they too have to learn how to use energy in order to make their presence known.

Each Soul Rescuer has their own way of moving Souls over and they are well versed in the above ways in which Spirit make themselves known.

There is a wide range of lost souls to rescue, and like counselling the living, the needs of a soul, and its requirements must be considered if you are to do your job properly.

Sometimes Soul Rescues have similarities, nevertheless no two are identical, and I treat each one with respect, and also as an individual case, you could think of it in the following context.

As a new baby entering this world its life is unique from when the child is born, there is no telling what its life will hold and when it will end. So when the time comes for the soul to return home, it will be unique too, depending on what the life of the individual was like, plus all those life
ingredients like karma, destiny, fate, personality etc
Another question you may ask is,
'Why do we need Soul Rescuers?'
There are many reasons like all workers of light we have a job to do, and as you are aware the world is in a bit of a mess and has been for quite a long while this has been happening for many, many years. It reached a stage that not everyone that dies is moving over peacefully, some are bound here for whatever reason. Some have gone to lower levels of existence, some religions call it hell.

We however, view it as a lower level of the astral ladder.

Some lower astral dwellers find their way back to our plain of existence, and can attach themselves to the living.

There are also the negative forces trying to undermine the good forces that are at work.

The balance of the planet and her vibrational levels are at risk especially in these times of change, some of humanity has not attained a grasp of what is going on and how all this is important to humanities survival.

Other reasons can be because, some people are full of ego and the material world, when death comes they do not want to go.

Some others are simply lost or confused, they may be looking for a loved one, some don't even realise that they are dead;

And the living can keep the dead here by their grieving for a loved one.

Some souls remain here to find a host on whom to feed their addictions, whether it is sex, drugs, or alcohol etc

There are many reasons why some souls do not find peace.

However, the majority of souls do find peace; and this problem has built up over a long period of time.

I believe everyone, should have a chance to return home to the light at some time.

Even if they have done something really bad, they do not move straight up the Astral Ladder it has to be achieved a rung at a time. Those of a darker nature have to face up to the consequences and be judged, and truly repentant, for their negative behavior or deeds.

Some will never return to the light, and some will attempt to escape from the lower realms in search of salvation and show remorse for past deeds.

Just as a matter of interest, I have often heard people say they wish they were psychic.

It's not all fun; it has its down sides.

One of the things I have heard them say is 'I would like to know what people think about me' that's fine if they like you.

I have picked up on people's thoughts that didn't like me or were jealous etc, it's very hurtful knowing the truth sometimes especially if they are not being genuine with you.

On one occasion when I was in my early stages of development I was on a trip in Scotland. I was in a tourist Information Centre and the man behind the counter had such hateful thoughts about me. I hadn't even spoken to him, he didn't even know me, and for the rest of the day I was so upset. I had no idea why he hated me.

I don't feel it is an advantage to know too much, the same can also be said when giving messages and predictions, think careful before you say what it is you can see or feel etc. If I told some of the people about the entities within their Aura that I trap and remove, it would cause them a great deal of anguish. Remember the passage I quoted from Lillian Beck's book - 'People are rarely able to handle it'. Well what if they could not deal with what you found out?

A great deal of care and forethought needs to be added.
I will give you an example and you can draw your own conclusion.

Remember the man who had his tongue cut out and was stoned in previous lives how it affected him in this life, how about the little dancer and her scholarship.

There was another case where a lady came for a massage and Reiki, and whilst having treatment she fell into a deep sleep. I then saw a small entity about the size of a baby its skin had a green hue about it; it was naked and showed no genitals. It had no nose to speak of, large eyes, and sharp teeth, and no body hair. It appeared between the woman's legs and tried desperately to claw its way into the woman's womb, I had never seen anything like this before. I pushed it away from her with light and it kept on returning to try again, I continued pushing it away from her.

I called in help from the Angels, and spirit Guides. It felt like only moments, then I became aware of two spirit presences approaching, I continued to work pushing the creature away with the light and Reiki symbols. I was not repelled by the creature's strange looks and concentrated on focusing love towards it. The two spirit beings took hold of the little baby like creature holding it by an arm each side of it and left carrying it away. The lady was unaware of what had happened. Had I have told her, there is no telling how she would have reacted.

I have worked with many such cases; I don't want to frighten you these incidents are not a daily occurrence.

Do remember, some Spirits are negative, they will offer you everything your heart desires to do their bidding, or encourage you to walk away from your spiritual path. There are also those who feed on human souls. Sounds just like a Hammer horror movie doesn't it?

Well they are not a very nice lot, so don't encourage them in. Never use an `Ouija' board, these open gateways to lower astral levels, and they can be difficult to get back. I only know of two people that can control a Ouija board safely.

I have lost count of the disorders that have occurred and the effort required to clean up after Ouija boards have been used in dwellings. It doesn't always just affect the house it's practiced in, but other dwellings within the vicinity as well.

Here is a story about one experience.

I was asked to assist Freya with a young man who had become terrified; he said a creature sat at the end of his bed. Sure enough there was a lower astral dweller of non-human origin; it wasn't actually too pleased to be on our plain.

The boy swore he had no idea where it came from, but my colleague soon discovered he wasn't being truthful. He had in fact been using an Ouija board for fun and had let the entity through. I often come across individuals who practiced just like the boy at a party for fun and many years later the entity is still attached to them within their aura. There are a number of cases where Ouija board users have been killed.

Another word of warning, don't dabble in black magic
either, for fun. And if you're dabbling with white magic be
very careful. White can turn grey and grey becomes black very
easily.

Those on the negative side are very strong, and as I have said I
have saved those stories and events for a later book. Negative
energies are real and these are not the worse cases I have come
across; if I could have filmed some of them they would make
very good movies.

In all things there has to be a balance. You can't have light
without dark, and believe me while fighting the dark; I have
had some very scary moments during my spiritual growth.
Hear in 2014 as I finish the last edit of this book. I still battle
and confront the darker forces, as instructed by Spirit. I have
total trust in the power of light there is not a glimmer of doubt
in my faith, if there was I would not be able to do my work
safely, and I would most definitely be with the men in white
coats, munching on a bag of jelly babies in the back of the
black van.

And so here I will lighten the atmosphere a little and tell you of
some of the first soul rescues, which took place in what now
seems such a long time ago.

The Scandinavian Warrior

As mentioned earlier, Spirits can attach themselves to the
living for a number of reasons. One time during a meditation
with the Nottingham group, I attracted a man who chose me
because I reminded him of his fiancée. I can't give you a date,
but I can tell you it was a time when the shores of England
were clean and un-spoilt, a time when there was no pollution,
no cars, factories or shops, no electric, telephones, or gas.

England really was a green and pleasant land. It was a time
going back to ancient history, when our shores were raided by
nations from across the sea. I found myself stood on a beach so
beautiful; my heart fills to bursting just remembering the scene.
The sun shone brightly, glistening on the sea, waves lapped
tenderly against the shore, a warm breeze caressed my skin, I
then became aware of strands of gingery fair hair blown by the
breeze across my cheek. My hair is long and dark and I realised
at this point I was sharing my body with the Spirit of a man.
I could feel myself within his body, I sensed his stature, he felt
six foot tall, broad shoulders and strong. I could feel he had a
thick untamed beard, his cheeks seemed tight from the salt air;
I then became aware of his emotions, his sadness, tears in his
eyes welling up, and the pain in his left forearm, which I knew
was broken, I felt his feelings of longing to go home.
At this point the group leader Vera brought us back to the
present in the group. I spoke of my situation, she told me his
name which I do not recall, and together we went back to
rescue him.
Vera could see hear and feel all that I and the lost Spirit could.
she told me to take him by the hand and within seconds we
were gliding across the sea heading towards grey mountains, I
could see a plateau and we landed there I was still holding his
hand and I led him to the center of the plateau. We could see a
light and a sky line, a hand appeared then the head of a young
woman peering around, her hair was long black and crinkled;
my personal thoughts were this is odd. I expected a
Scandinavian fair haired type.
I could hear Vera talking to me, she told me to let go of his
hand and take two steps back, I could feel all his emotions of
love for her, he turned from me and walk towards the light.
I took two more steps back then I turned back towards the sea
and felt myself gliding across clear water and the lush
greenness of our beautiful un-spoilt English countryside. I was

sensing how good it felt to be home and an over whelming love for those who I had been waiting for me, for so long. On my return back to the group, I found I was wearing a spiritual golden bangle on my left wrist, when he gave it to me I don't recall, but I still am aware that it is there. Sometimes spirit, give us gifts, they are from their dimension that is why we are able to see them spiritually but not physically.

The Rights of Passage

A young boy came to me or should I say a young man, in his culture he was of the age when he must undergo the rights of passage to become a man. An Aborigine boy came to me and I felt I was like a mother figure to him. He held me closely, and I returned his affection. Beginning to sense there was something wrong, he did not speak. He just held onto me tightly, I told him he could stay as long as he wished, and the mother, son bond felt stronger, as if he was my own child. Later that night I began to feel ill, a loud noise filled my head which would not stop, my heart raced and pounded in my chest. I felt as though I was dying. My partner lay asleep by my side. While I shared the feelings and emotions of the young boy and I knew these were his last moments in his short life. It was a surreal feeling being in both worlds, I just knew I was going to die. I fell asleep, and as I awoke every sound around me was so very loud, it vibrated at a high frequency. As this continued each sound became more and more distant, as the last beats of my heart labored, and the sounds became remote. I felt peaceful, floating away as the sounds faded. Within an instant I was back wide awake and perfectly normal, I looked around the dimly lit bedroom as dawn broke its first rays of light onto the window, the young boy had left as suddenly as he had come, and he had relived his death and had now moved over peacefully.

I feel quite emotional as I write this story, I never knew his name, and I hope one day he will be reunited with his mother. He obviously missed her, when he was alone and dying. At least I was able to be a substitute when he needed her.

The Lost Soldier

I found myself in the cold and dark, in a small yellow dingy, the sea bobbing up and down like a cork rhythmically. I could see two men in life jackets lying in the dingy.

A shaft of golden light fell from the sky on to one of the men and he floated up into it, but then he struggled and was reluctant to go, I reached for his hand and went with him. We stood in the light and he removed his wet clothes. I saw a dog tag around his neck, but I was not given a name, a pair of hands gave me a warm robe, and a pair of thick wooly socks. He put these on and seemed calmer, 'Look into the light, what you see' I was told to say.

A carousel appeared, the horses going up and down and round and round. Then we heard a voice saying, 'Life goes around and around, up and down but never stops'

We climbed onto the carousel laughing, the happiness was overwhelming, round and round we went like children laughter ringing out, there was such joy. As we rode the carousel he began to draw more and more distant from me till I could see him no more. The carousel was still turning, and then a pair of arms lifted me off like a child, I was told it was time to go back. I found myself in the cold and darkness of the dingy and the rhythmical bobbing of the ocean. I looked for the second man, but he was nowhere to be seen, I had expected to take

him up next. It was very likely to have been a Guardian
Spirit waiting with him until he was rescued.
We all have a Guardian Angel looking after us.

The Return of a King

Ok so it's not 'Lord of the Rings', but another interesting
rescue journey for me. As I connected I became aware of a
very heavy metal band around my head. And I was then
approached by a man wearing a crown. He was dressed in 14th
century clothing and wore a red tunic and leggings with a
leather belt. At some point we took hold of each other's hand,
and he began to lead me down dark damp passages, moss's and
algae clung to the walls, and he held a torch high to guide our
way, we went through many doors and passage ways and I felt
the incline as we traveled along. I presumed we were going to
the battlements, but something wasn't quite right, he was
leading me and not I him.
When we reached our destination he opened a large wooden
door, we were not at the battlements. However, there in front
of us was a level of light which exists between heaven and
earth, the light was tremendously bright, much brighter than
any soul rescue light I had seen before. Another doorway
opened within it, even brighter than the previous one, but it did
not hurt our eyes. We stood holding hands, and I was aware
someone had come for him. He turned to face me looking into
my eyes with tenderness, 'Come with me', he said softly. I
knew what lay on the other side of the door and wanted to go,
but I also knew I could not.
Like a flash of thunder, I was literally whisked away at such
speed there was not even time to blink. Down the darkness of
the passages, and right the way back to the here and now. I felt
so alone; this soul rescue is one that pulls at the heart strings
for a different reason.

The Home Coming

He just appeared in front of me. There was so much fear in his eyes; I must admit I have never seen anyone so afraid. Our eyes are said to be the windows to the soul, of which I have found to be true, this poor man's soul was in great torment. I took hold of his hand, and turned to walk him to the doorway of light. I was sure it would appear as it had done so many times before. As I waited it did not appear, in its place were grey clouds, they began to part, reveling to my surprise a scene from the 1940s, with singing and music. Beer was flowing, pint glasses filled to the brim, a piano played, people stood singing and the cigarette smoke was so thick it was like a London fog; people were laughing and having a jolly good time. Without so much as a glance, the soldier ran past me and into the bar, people welcomed him, but that wasn't all a stream of soldiers filed past me like an Inter-City125 train running after him as fast as their legs could carry them laughing and shouting. This was the home coming they wanted, and I am sure deserved.

The Biker

A new client came for a massage and as I worked, I became aware of a very strong energy; my shoulder and arm became crooked and painful and a young man dressed in motor bike leathers appeared. I told him he would have to wait until I had finished, and asked him to stop the pain, which he did. He sat in the chair and waited. After the treatment and my family duties were done, I sat in the treatment room with him, calling in the light and guiding Spirits. Within moments I was at one with the young man, aware of his stature and his feelings.

He told me his name was David Richardson, and then he proceeded to take me to the night of his death. It was a dark autumn evening, torrential rain hitting the bike and its rider with force. I could see David on his motor bike, the spray of water slashing across the red rear lights. I then at this point, found myself riding pillion on the bike, speeding through the rain and the darkness. But at no point did I feel unsafe. The darkness then gave way to a misty light, and I found myself stood in the road, the bike lay on its side. As I peered into the darkness, I became aware that someone else was there that night with David, although I had not been aware of them until now.

I could only see a white helmet and nothing more. I walked out towards it, and was told it was David's sister Sally Anne.

I sensed a strong connection with her parents their grief was not only over whelming but also holding her back from returning to the light. She felt she couldn't leave them, so would not go. There was a light to my left becoming brighter; Sally said she could not leave her parents. At this point within the light came an old gentleman, he called to her by name, on seeing him the energy's changed, a strong feeling of love filled all of us to the brim. With arms out stretched she reach out to him, he took hold of her hands and indicated it was time to go. The three of them turned and walked away, the light closed behind them. I was left alone standing in the road, with only the darkness and the rain for company.

Eventually my Spirit energy came back to my body.

I then duly carried on with my evening chores.

This was the first time I had experienced a spirit brought to me for rescue in the aura of a client.

Development wise this was my next step.

When my client next came for a treatment he remarked how good he had felt after treatment. But I did not tell him about the Spirit he had brought with him on his last visit.

Why David had chosen him I do not know. But hopefully
their parents can also now move on.

A women who lived in Victorian times, she was in her early
thirty's and she stood scrubbing washing, on a rubbing board,
she looked at me and showed me her hands they were red and
sore. We then found ourselves stood in a cobbled street, she
turned to look at me once more, and we both looked up to, a
leaded window which was open in a building high on the roof
of an old house, on the opposite side of the street. Light
streamed forth and we simply floated up holding hands. She
had found peace at last.
I hope if she has reincarnated she has a `state of the art'
washing machine.

I found myself in at Maidenhead Castle in the County Dorset.
I am not much of an historian but those kind people who cater
for tourists like me, had placed some very informative
information boards for us to look at as we moved around the
castle. But having a memory like a colander for history, you
will have to forgive my lack of historical fact. I prefer to call
them `senior moments' of which there are quite a few.
There is little left of Maidenhead Castle, it dates back to pre-
roman times and you can see shapes where homes and defenses
had been all those centuries ago. As I walked my way up a
grassy track I sensed the change in energies which is nothing
unusual. I felt as though, I was stood on a burial ground
although there was no information to support my theory.
There were many well-worn paths generated by the never
ending streams of visitors. Although I felt I would go along
one path because it was easy on the old leg muscles, spirit had
other ideas and I found myself walking the path they had
chosen for me. I knew they would have their reasons for
sending me this way, so off I went. As I walked I felt my back

straighten and my shoulders pulling back, as I am ashamed
to say I'm a slouchier. All that time of walking with a book on
my head as a child was in vain. So with my new found straight
and upright posture, I became taller and also aware that a large
number of spirits were beginning to follow me. My straight
shouldered companion made himself known to me. I sensed a
feeling of authority and a man of pride filtered through me, at
his side walked his nineteen year old daughter, a long mousey
brown plait lay at her left shoulder. They all followed me, in
silence no names were given no words spoken and no
information just silence.

I completed my tour, and headed back to the B & B. retiring
for the night. I drifted off to sleep, no wiser about my new and
very quiet companions.

The next morning I had just woken up, when the young women
with the long plait, sat by my side. She then took me along to
her home where people were mourning the loss of someone
dear to them. At this point our bodies merged, and I became
aware of all her feelings. She showed me a morning when she
woken inside the stone hut it was gloomy, cold, but dry, hay
littered the floor, a musty smell lingered on the air, the dawn
was breaking and the early morning light poked its way
through the gap in the stone work which acted like a window.
I became aware of a man lying next to me, it was her father.
In the gloom of the morning he spoke to her he said he would
kill her himself, before they could have her, she smiled
reassuring at him. She then proceeded to tell him that her
illness would take her first. Why she chose to show me this, I
do not know but it was important to her and if just showing me
helped them then, this is all I would wish for. They all
followed me around for three days and then melted away, I
hope to the light.

I will not take much more of your time with more soul
rescue stories, for now there have been hundreds each one as
special as the next and they can vary in detail and complexity.
These were some of my early ones, and the experiences led me
on to a new level of development and understanding. But
before I end the chapter I must keep a promise to
James Frances or Frank as he was known,
James Frances's came to me, not for soul rescue but for another
reason. He came from Spirit and was dressed in khaki shorts
and shirt. He looked at me with his bright blue eyes his
sunburnt face peering out from under his sandy brown hair.
I could feel his parched throat, and dry mouth, his wish for
more water to quench his thirst as the heat was rising from the
desert sands.
The left side of his face was badly sunburnt and scarred.
He then showed me a photograph of himself, before the war.
He was a handsome young man hair combed back, bright blue
happy eyes, and his beloved pipe, he said he felt so forgotten;
all he asked of me was to remember him. He then showed me a
notebook, and then proceeded to produce a modern
Dictaphone. I thanked him and promised I would never forget
him.
What was the reason for showing me a notebook and a
Dictaphone?
Every day before going to sleep I wrote notes about that day's
experience. However at that time my life's circumstances had
changed, and time was at a premium. So he was telling me to
get a Dictaphone, and I did. It made life so much easier.
So James Francis, this is for you, hear you are in black and
white. Remembered for always, just as I promised!

When Spirits Move In

Most of my work involves Spirits in some shape or form, whilst some come to help me do my work, or work through me; there are others who are held here in this dimension for whatever reason. There can be many reasons, why they are unable to move over as I have said in a previous chapter. Spirits can be held here by loved ones who just can't let them go. Like in Sally and Richards case.
If someone you love passes over; light a candle, burn incense, say prayers tell them how much you love them, give them permission to go to the light. Give them your blessing and set them free. This applies to pets as well.

Spirits are often unwilling to move over when they find the house they lived in has a new occupier, especially when the new owner starts to put their stamp on the property. Modernising, extending even re-decorating can trigger a haunting; even the bravest of non-believers have called me in when a chisel flew across the room on its own into a gas pipe.

I had this experience with a house I bought in 2000

The old lady who had occupied the property had passed away in her nineties and was not too pleased to find someone else living in her home. She had spent her last few weeks of her life at her daughter's and the house I had bought had been empty for some time, but it was still her home, even though she had not died there. If she had died there, maybe her moving would not have been delayed. She also didn't like changes to her home when she was alive let alone when she was dead. Nevertheless the house needed some work doing and the first job was to make the garden secure for my partners dog. Lots of trees and bushes had to be removed and the old lady made it quite clear she was not happy; I was made to feel very unwelcome in the house especially when I arrived home from work. The last thing I needed was an unfriendly welcome. As unbeknown to me I had Fibromyalgia as well as arthritis, as a result of this I was feeling quite ill and at times and low on patience. When I worked out what the problem in the house was, I told her quite simply she was dead, in as gentle a way as possible, and I had bought the house after she had passed away. I promised her I would take good care of it and make her a garden she could be proud of. I also told her she was welcome to visit any time she wanted to. It seemed to do the trick, and she moved over.

A few weeks later I came home from work I was in a bad mood, and in pain. The old lady appeared. In my grumpy state of mind I was none too pleasant 'What the *** are you doing here' She looked straight at me and said softly, 'I've come to say good bye' she said quite meekly to me. She had found her husband who had died some years previously, he stood by her side and must have been thinking I was a right dragon.

I apologised for my behavior explaining I had just had a really bad day. I also told them, I would keep my promise and they were always welcome. I felt just as guilty at being grumpy towards them even though they were dead, I would have felt just as bad if they had been alive.

They came back now and again, when we were undergoing any major work, even my partner used to say I feel like someone is here. 'Yes it's the old lady just coming to have a look' It became a bit of a joke, every time we did anything I would say what I was going to do and hoped she would approve.

There have been many documented cases of spirits not wanting to leave their homes, and still being emotionally attached to something in their home or on their land.

There are spirits that haunt the same place over and over again, like a video tape playing. They are in fact carrying out a task or their last act, just before there death, plain crashes, accidents, battles all leave their vibrational mark on the land, sometimes they are looking for loved ones or just reliving a traumatic event. These poor spirits need setting free. How would you like to live the same thing over and over again for all eternity?

I often had spirit children staying with me. Normally they would come to me via a client or friend attached in their aura. I would give the client or friend a treatment and this detached the spirit from them to me. Then I make a point of keeping the spirit with me until they have gone so they cannot become reattached. I would then work with the spirit until someone came to move them over.

There are some Spirits that are trapped by jealousy, or do not want to give up their mortal lives and personal possessions. There are those who were fond of earthly pleasures, and are reluctant to leave them behind, it may be that they were fond of drink, drugs, gambling or sex etc. Yes there are randy spirits that will jump in at any opportunity for a quick knee trembler. They connect to their chosen host's aura; then share the thrills of the host as he/she undertakes pleasure of his/her recreational pursuit.

I have experienced this first hand my partner at the time had picked up an amorous spirit.

I wasn't aware at first that this attachment had taken place, but sensed a change in his lovemaking. I wondered but didn't pay much attention, and then on occasions I sensed the change in his kiss. One evening, when I returned home from the Nottingham group, he kissed me it didn't feel right, looking into his eyes I could see the attachment. 'How are you feeling' I asked he thought for a moment, 'Actually now you come to mention it I do feel strange' he said. I told him about his attachment and proceeded to remove it. The male spirit attached to him was none too pleased to be discovered, and I need to remove him I knew full well this type wouldn't go willingly with a nice counseling chat; So I set him a challenge, if he succeeded in the challenge he could stay, if not he must go. He accepted feeling very sure of himself. However, I knew I would win, which I did, and he promptly left.

I did meet one lady who also had an amorous spirit living with her, no socks under the bed and no one to look after; it was a mutual arrangement which she was quite happy with.

Wandering spirits need to move over, persuading them to go, can be difficult, convincing them that they are dead with compassion and thoughtfulness, even more so. The spirits that guide me are well aware of their weak areas or points of conversation that will strike a cord and so they can be convinced they need to move on. For the most part, once they are aware that there is something better they tend to leave willingly. I always tell them if you don't like it you can always come back, what have you got to lose? As yet no one has ever returned.

As a Soul Rescuer my main job was to help lost or wandering Spirits to find their way home and in some cases like in the soul rescue stories, I take them to the last exit from this life to the next, this is the final point that my spirit Guides will allow me to go. There have been times when I have wanted to go too, like with the king in the soul rescue chapter. I know what is there in my heart and mind but I cannot tell you because words will not allow me to.

When the lost spirits reach their destination, I can honestly say with my hand on my heart that there is a great feeling of peace, calm and often relief.

Those that come to meet them give off a feeling of love that I can only compare with some of the angelic encounters, I have experienced it and it is so powerful, it makes you cry with joy.

There are some spiritual people who only work with the living and don't see the dead as important. The dead to me are more than vibrations of things gone by; they are living beings in another form, who deserve just as much help as we mortals. Just because the majority of people can't see them doesn't mean they don't have a right to help.

I have met people who say the dead are not important, and not to soul rescue, these were people very high up in spiritual standing. I was so shocked by their dismissive attitude, when they were in fact of high spiritual rank and actually teaching others.

Also I don't know, why I can move from one world to another, with such ease, for me it is as simple as stepping across a white line in the road, I can be in both worlds at the same time, or deep within the other realms, when it is safe to do so.

In my early days of growth I also wondered why; if someone comes to take you home what is the reason for so many wandering spirits in need of rescue, and why don't children go straight away too; as they are in essence innocent.

Perhaps it is because these dead follow the living around they are unable to see their fellow spirits.

Attracted to the light like moths to a lantern they circle around, trapped in a state of living death, until Spirit Guides and helpers show them the way home.

Exorcism is another form of soul rescue used on a religious level; this is a method that should be used with great care. Exorcising your great aunt Flo for example, can cause more aggravation, love and light and persuasion is what is needed; not banishing them to the darkness which some exorcists do. In the darkness they cannot heal, so you're not helping them at all.

Yes there are demon type entities and I have done battle a few times whilst doing my work. Nevertheless I always offer them a chance to return to the light first, before I deal with them.

This is my personal way of working.

You may also have seen on television, spirits moving things around, they can do this.

The telephone can also be used by spirit. Electricity is energy and can be used, the stories you have heard of the dead ringing up are true. Electricity can be easily manipulated by them; often a sign of spirit activity can be the results of lots of popped light bulbs and broken electrical appliances.

Before you start thinking Aunty Flo has come back to haunt you check the logical first. Are you're electrics safe, and how old is the appliance and the light bulbs, have you had electrical surges etc.

Keep a healthy degree of skepticism, it is a good thing and it will help you keep a balanced outlook on life.

Poltergeist type energies are very good at manipulating energies of an electrical nature as well as moving objects.

They need to be where there is strong energies to draw on, some poltergeist like to tidy up unfortunately they're few and far between, I have never met one and I wouldn't mind one or two of those kind myself.

They are often reported where teenagers are, not surprising, as teenagers go through so much trauma, with their hormonal systems whizzing all over the place, mental and physical changes taking place at this time.

The feelings that the parents don't understand them, some parents find the children they love so much driving them so far up the wall, that they get to a point that they actually dislike their own kids.

Normally everything balances out but in some cases it can result in a child leaving home before they were really ready to do so.

Amongst the routine of adult life's ups and downs and the negativity generated by a household, can be an excellent source to draw on, by a poltergeist. They can feed on the energy and make themselves known by throwing their weight around.

With love and understanding you can get through your families ups and downs. If you suspect spiritual activity, then call in a medium, or Soul Rescuer to check things out for you.

Remember negative energies don't like nice energies; it weakens their grip. So try to generate positive energies in your home, and a cleansing ritual will also help.

Any parent with a light heart can watch the sketches of Harry Enfield's, 'Kevin' and smile.......they know exactly what I mean.

Some Words of Wisdom

Sharing with Others

You will find it is advisable when you have discovered your
abilities not to tell everyone you meet. As an example if I said
to my employer over a tea break, 'I talk to dead people, and I
take their soul's home, and then I come back again.'
While he was sending, for the men in white coats, to come and
collect me, think about what I said to him. It sounds completely
crazy. However, I can also explain it all away like a
psychiatrist too.
Even now after all that has happened, I can still see the men in
white coats point of view.
Everyone is born with the ability to work with psychic energy.
After all as the advert goes 'It's the appliance of science.'
If you do find yourself telling just anybody you will get a very
mixed bag of responses. Some will think you are unhinged;
some will be afraid of you.
This is something which I have experienced, I have found
people with very strict religious beliefs, fall into latter
category. At an introduction to healing day, I spent a great deal
of time convincing a family whose mum had become a
Reverend that, 'I don't do the work for the devil.' Eventually
she understood, when I said 'I am of the light, and not
everybody can follow the same belief system'
There are others that will laugh at you; some will ignore you.
Some will instantly say 'OK, what am I thinking,' and want
you to perform on the spot for them, like a side show.
If you are able to do that, so well and good it will give them
either something to think about or scare them half to death.
The majority of people will listen and then perhaps start to tell
you about some experience they or someone else has had. You

will instinctively know who is of like mind, and who will
have you popped promptly into a straightjacket.

I have been very fortunate, to have been shown many facets of
spiritual life, and the way people respond to their newly
acquired gifts or abilities.

One the pleasurable experience for me is to watch individual's
open up and grow and their mind energy widen. It is so very
special for me, like seeing a beautiful flower unfolding it
petals.

There are numerous ways for you to work and many ways of
working. You may even be on a personal quest, healing karmic
patterns, learning valuable life lessons, many of you have been
reincarnated here for a reason. Some of your vibrations are
needed to heal the planet, and help mankind through the
transition.

For most of us it is about helping others and raising planetary
vibrations. Whatever you channel you act by your own free
will. If you don't want to carry on developing or working with
energy that is fine too, it's your choice. No one will force you.
You need to be aware that you also have to ask spirit for help
when you need it, they are not allowed to interfere with your
life. This is one of the spiritual laws, Diana cooper has written
a book on the spiritual laws.

It is your life. Ask if you need some guidance or help from the
spirits of light. Remember to always state, 'For my highest
good,' and trust the process. Even if it seems not to be working
the way you intended.

They will find a way that is best for you, and if you wait long
enough even if it's not the way you planned it you will see the
end result was worth it. Patience is an important lesson we all
learn. Spirit, work in their own way; and in their own time
frame. They actually do know what is best.

I have friends who have just as much ability as mine and some who have much more.

They have eventually come to a point after a disturbing event in their lives; that they have decided not to continue with this path anymore.

It's not easy to follow, one close friend in particular will tell you, 'Life sucks' and this is a clip from her story,

Freya, is a white witch she has had to overcome hurdle after hurdle, and it has been an uphill struggle. She is quite capable of casting spells that can put some people in very difficult circumstances. She has been known to put lights out in a superstore and sets security alarms off.

Keeping white is not as easy as you may think, and you have the 'reap what you sow' law to think about. Which is a spiritual law, and it applies to many paths, it simply means in pagan and witch laws, what you give out you get back three times, good or bad, hence the term, three fold.

There have been many battles for her over time, and she often feels like throwing down her broomstick and jumping all over it, and on occasions she has. Nevertheless she always comes out fighting and I must admit I am very proud of her. She is still a white witch, after all that has happened.

Dark forces have almost thrown her off the pier, and when my life was being threatened by dark forces, Freya was the one who saved me. I was in another country at the time, which gives you a little insight into how powerful she is.

Freya earned the respect of a powerful Spirit witch who had been working with me for some time, called Raven.

Raven in her life on earth, was a witch like Freya.

However, she found herself on the dark side through love of a man who was not of the light. Raven was a case of white going grey and then black, she worked on the dark side for many centuries, and she is now still in the world of spirit and in the process of atoning for some of her misdemeanors in her past life. So she is well aware of how hard the Wiccan, and magic path can be.

If the world of the dark ones attained Freya as their own, they would class this as a great triumph and this is why they target her and she has to watch what she says, for example if someone has treated her unjustly the thought is the deed, and in kicks the three fold law, white, gray, black so easily created. I am of the mind the harder the path the more powerful and stronger your abilities will be.

It has been an uphill struggle but I'm happy to report her seemingly impossible dream of moving to the north coast took fourteen years to manifest with so many almost there times and then falling apart at the last minute, then as if a magic wand had been waved her dream house appeared with in less than a week it was hers with everything she wanted and her back garden is the sea and sand.

Her path has also changed as she is now a sea witch working with the sea fey and sea energy's healing the sea and its wild life.

I have found a number of cases were the darker forces will try to alter your path or stop it, however eventually the darker forces do relent when they feel they can't find a way in to your armor, this is why they tend to strike when you are feeling low, unhappily lonely depressed, you're not getting what you think you want, when your heart has been broken or when life's ups and downs are troubling you.

At this point you are vulnerable. It's your Achilles heel.

So I recommend you find your vulnerable spots and become aware of them or it.

When you are having a tough time, have faith call in the light forces and remember, the more of an impact you can make for the light, sometimes the harder you may get hit by negative forces from the lower astral realm

Family and Friends

I think we need to stop hear for a moment, and consider our family and friends.

This may be an issue or can become one, but don't let it stop your growth. If they love you they will let you be free to be the person you truly are, even if they don't understand.

It may be a case that you are perhaps hiding your feelings because others may not understand or be like you. It's not an easy situation to be in.

Their needs may overshadow your own. But remember no second is wasted when working with spiritual matters, no matter how small every second counts. Try to find a way to integrate it into your life.

I used to meet many over the years, who thought, I'm short of a few bails, that my beliefs are completely crazy.

At first it bothered me, I also felt frustrated that they didn't understand; I felt sad that they were missing out on a whole new world. I found I eventually didn't mind what others thought or think of me. I may have been nick named Angie my weird friend and such like, I used to laugh and pass a funny comment, and just let it go.

I have also stood by and watched people laugh at me, so much so that they almost found themselves standing in a puddle and in needed of a change of underwear, and others that would quite happily watch me burn at the stake. .

I know the truth, and one day when they reach the time when they move over they will know the truth; that there is so much more to life than the material world.

I sometimes feel sad that there are so many who will miss out on the richness of this fascinating world that few get a glimpse off.

Another thing you can do is to adapt your conversation or practices in front of others, if you know it will distress them, it can be as simple as not talking about something that upsets or unsettles them.

When my world of spirit opened up I wanted to shout from the roof tops to every one 'look at this it's amazing, and I wanted everyone to experience the beautiful side of this world for themselves I wanted them to see the angels and the world of the light spirits and show everyone how they interact with us, and for them not to be afraid of death.'

On such occasions you need to show empathy, understanding and respect their difference, whilst trying to remain true to your beliefs. It's a two way thing you know. Remember patience is a virtue we all should strive for.

I have found because some people have not been confronted directly with spiritual matters, in time they start to ask questions and become more open, especially if they were afraid of some aspects such as, death for example.

Now in 2014 I find many people are open minded and there's a mass movement of human conscious energy, bring people together, and yet there are religious forces and belief system's that believe we are been fooled by the dark ones, However if you know the passages from the bible you will find there is enough evidence to show we are working in the name of light the way the bible says, even though many light workers are in fact not christens.

Children

It can be difficult if you have children who are not on the same wavelength, it can be embarrassing for them, and they may wish you to keep your spiritual life under wraps. Respect their wishes, if they just accept you are what you are then that is a blessing in its self.

Your children may be gifted but don't want to use it.

Don't pressure them, having a parent that understands their differences is a wonderful gift in itself, they should be free to enjoy their youth and time spend growing up. Being able to make their own choices, it is their rite of passage in life.

There can be difficulties, especially if the parents are separated, they may find themselves torn between two completely different views of life. One parent may follow a spiritual path and the other parent may have a totally different view on life.

I think the best way to deal with this situation, is to just accept the differences and not force your points of view. Ideally neither parent should criticize the other, but respect the fact that no two people are alike. Whilst at the same time being true to their own values.

Be as open, as you can be, and honest, but not forceful, and show consideration for each other, and especially around young children. You might be flying high on your spiritual broomstick and enjoying the ride. However, please, please be aware of what you say in front of them, they are so easily influenced, and frightened. They are children and may place their own interpretation on conversations they have overheard, and although your child may be gifted, they should be allowed to enjoy their childhood and not have the pressures of spiritual nature dominating their world. When they tell you something of a spiritual nature listen to what they have to say, often these young souls have been here before and wise words can come out of their young minds.

The child in your life will find his or her own way, and choose for themselves how they view life, God and the universe, and they may grow into something very different from you.

In the early days I would only make my feelings known, if any of my children were participating in any belief system which was dangerous, unsafe, or controlling.

I have boundaries, no Ouija boards, or magic of any negative nature, their abilities must never be used to cause harm to others or be used selfishly.

Does that make me a controlling parent? I wish only to keep them safe as I see too many cases of young people who have been victims of negative practices, in the name of fun.

Now many years down the line my children accept what I am and the work I do. However, I never pressure or ask them to become involved, even though they both are gifted and one views it very differently to me; I understand where he is coming from.

If they wish to become involved in a session or group they can, and on odd occasions did of their own accord. A child Will take what they need and potter off on their own particular path. Children need space and time to experience life, when they are ready to grow spiritually, they will find the watering can and be led to the right people at the right time just like you and I were. If that is the path they choose or were born for. Putting pressure on them and their gifts can be damaging, remember, Lillian Becks book 'Many can't handle it and become unstable......' be very aware if you are responsible for these children........

I have seen many young people and children who have been made to follow their parent's belief system and given no freedom of choice, it is understandable that parents will do this. In the same way I would try, to stop my children getting involved in any negative spiritual activity. It is no different to advising or trying to stop your children taking drugs, or committing offences etc.

However, no child should be forced or conditioned into a practice they do not feel is right for them.

I have come across children who quote to me word for
word their parents beliefs, and one man in his early twenty's,
who said that he didn't to listen to pop music because his
parents said it was music the devil had made to lure people in.
How easily influenced these young growing minds are.
The new age beliefs I follow, allow a young person to find
their own way, knowledge is available, and questions answered
honestly, giving them an open mind on what other people
believe in, tolerance, wisdom and understanding.
Then ultimately they make the choice of the path they take.
Should they ask a question and if you don't know the answers
say you don't know. Or possibly you could find the answer by
working together,

Like many belief systems we believe love and light is strong
and powerful. We should accept one another and not harm
anyone with our beliefs, allow them to grow and see that life
goes beyond the world of the computer, TV and violence.

That life can be a rich and wonderful experience.

The Astral Ladder

You have heard me mention the Astral Ladder many times; our belief system does not have heaven at the top and hell at the bottom with us in the middle.

We view it as a type of vibrational ladder, so if you imagine the very top rung up would be say God, Allah, the universal force, or the highest ranking alien life form, whatever you believe in. Now each rung down, from there contains a form of life force energy or being, so Angels will be high up the ladder, Avatars, Prophets, high ranking Spirits like Ascended Masters, and all those kinds of light beings. So as we work our way down the ladder we have other kinds of Spirit entities, Earth Angels, Reincarnates, Light Workers, Star Children, holy people, Hathors, and Spirits that have passed over but work with us, proving there is life after death. Healing Spirits, Guiding Sprits and a whole range of beings, you could maybe imagine the rungs been very wide and all types of light beings, who are of the same or similar vibrations side by side, the quote from the bible

'In my house there are many mansions' comes to mind.

Just a thought, All these faiths and beliefs that we humans have with regards to God, Goddesses Allah etc, could theses not also be viewed as mansions, all under one roof like different flats ? Regardless of whom we feel is god head or what we believe in, by whatever name we call it or worship it.

Were all under one roof !

I cannot tell you where everyone is or what rung they are on. But you can be sure they are all there, I guess you could call it a spiritual hierarchy.

Humans are somewhere around the middle, and if you advance in spiritual growth then you move up a rung, until eventually you don't have to be reincarnated. You may even be at a phase in your growth where you can return to your source from where you came originally,

To become lower down the Astral Ladder, you need to do things that are not acceptable, that are negative.

The lower you go down the Astral Ladder I have found the less of a human form an entity has.

I have established through my experiences when moving and clearing negative lower astral dwellers, in some instances the amount of light applied have been known to make a human fall out of a casing of black energy, which looked something similar to black solidified tar.

They also vary in shapes and forms, depending on where they dwell, and it is not uncommon for them to look like something out of a horror movie with fangs and yellow eyes and smelling none too fresh. Their appearance can be anything from seething rivers of black to full fire and brimstone types. When I am working with these Spirits I do not feel afraid, and it does not trouble me, this is because I have faith and love in the light and no doubts in the power of light forces to overcome dark forces..........

There are many cases and events recorded related to these lower astral dwellers, some have been moved into what can only be described as a sort of waiting area where they will work with spirits, who are at a level of ability to deal with them. It may be that the lower dweller wishes to move up and are sorry for whatever they did wrong.

I have come across some who said they wanted to move upward, but were in fact thinking it would get them out of trouble when their souls were coming to be collected.

Or try to hide by saying they wanted help when they don't really. It's just a way of getting you to lower your guard and to get you to let them in.

They can be quite plausible at times, and it's then that you have to remain confident and astute in your beliefs and abilities.

However, the positive aspect of the Astral Ladder is if you are going up, you will become lighter and lighter in vibration and you will have learned what you needed to and will not have to return unless you're going to help those on the earth plain.

Reincarnation

So much has been written about reincarnation, I have no doubts that we are able to be reincarnate, if it is necessary, or it is our wish too.

The new age has brought with it many reincarnations from higher up the Astral Ladder to the earth plain over a number of years. Over history there have been many prophets, sages and wise men and women, bringing knowledge, wisdom, and blessings in many shapes and forms to help mankind.

Mother Merra is one as you may recall she helped me in the first stages of my awakening after I had almost taken my life, you can even go and visit her and sit with her.

The last few decades has seen a increase of Light Workers, Star Children, Indigo Children, Crystal Children, Earth Angels, to name but a few, many old souls are awakening, and contributing light and love in their own way. The reason behind the reincarnations of these beings' is to do with the planetary balance.

It is a very in-depth topic which will take you into quantum physics, vibrational frequencies, time and space, and would probably sound a little like a Stephen Hawkins book. But for this book, I will explain the basic scheme of things of our belief system. As a more in depth topic it will be explained in 'Phoenix in flight' a future book.

The world is out of balance, and Mother Earth can't take much more, for hundreds of years, war, greed, doctrine, power, and negative events have tipped the balance in favor of negative, or evil. Whatever you wish to call it, and so we are in need of intervention if planet earth is to survive, or should I say we survive, there have been many living creatures before us and they died out too, earth would in that instance cleanse and heal, what life form would survive or be born I have no idea.

I do know that this is the first time that this opportunity for mankind to continue his existence has occurred and that was part of a message channeled from spirit some time ago, .

The balance must be re-addressed. And these incarnates play a major role in the new world to come, mother earths vibrational field is becoming much higher and if we are to survive we must also become higher in vibrational light.

In our past there was a balance of good and evil or negative, (higher vibrations and lower vibrations) good having the upper hand, as a result the negative has grown, there are many high ranking people of the dark and not the light, we have seen an increase of horrifying things happening. Mother Earth absorbs all the negative energy from these events in the form of vibrational frequencies. Hence the increase in floods, earth quakes, hurricanes, tsunamis' etc.

Think of it as if you ate something that didn't agree with your stomach, what is likely to happen?

We also affect our world with all our actions, and no longer live in harmony with nature. Even the body which we live in was not designed to live the life style we do.

Consequently, more and more people are developing reactions and allergies, to foods, chemicals and a whole range of bi products from modern society, causing mental and physical health problems. We have so much preservative in our body's, that when we die, our bodies are in fact taking, much longer to decompose, we are in the ground, and become part of the food chain for the insect life, I wonder how do our dead body's affect them.

With the planet so out of balance, this has to be addressed. One way this is being achieved, is that certain Spirits and old souls from many realms of the astral ladder, are now playing their part by being reincarnated to help mankind, and Mother nature. These new incarnates teach love and light, and awaken others to their spiritual path. There is an increase in shamans and

pagans and earth natured people, who return to ancient
ancestral ways, the ancients were in tune with nature, they
sensed the spirits; they knew of the life after death, they were
able to use energy to heal as they were intuitive.

There are people who work at high vibratory levels in order to
bring more light to the earth, to connect and awaken more
people, and so many more people working in their own way, it
is like a vast web we are all connected.

Over the years we had lost that ancient connection in our fast
moving and growing society, we are told what we should do,
what we should think, and even how we should pray, and who
we should pray to, how we should dress, what we should eat.
Man controls other men in his quest, rapes and ravages mother
earth for material wealth, and not always for knowledge, but in
the race for material goods and greed, to control others, and for
power. And for those who remembered the way and stayed in
tune with light and nature, they were persecuted in one way or
another, branded as heretics, witches, devil worshippers and
the enemy.

The connection to the source of light is now being actively
encouraged and embraced by more and more people.

The evidence of life after death is clear, to all who open their
eyes. Awareness, of the fact there is more to life, than the
material wants and needs, mankind is realising exactly just how
fragile Mother Nature really is and that she needs tender loving
care to help her recover. Many people strive and fight to stop
the negative thoughts and behavior towards earth, and these
urban warriors, should be commended for standing up and
fighting,

In helping mother earth we help ourselves. As we connect once
more to the abilities we had many years ago much is being
relearned, our intuition sharpens, we become more sensitive,
and also more self-aware, braver to do something to help our
world and not stick our heads in the sand, while life goes on

around us, having more courage to stand out from the
crowd and grow into all that we can be.

Those who have reincarnated to help others, teach, and pass on
their knowledge, and more children are now being allowed to
develop as they should, those imaginary friends are now often
recognised by spiritual parents as real friends from the spirit
World, the evidence that we live on after death in another form
is vast,
Our physical body is just a shell, we are here to learn and grow;
so we can move forward working through Karma, learning,
growing and so advance up the Astral Ladder step by step this
in turn raises the planetary vibration, being in tune with Mother
Earth in her move forward and assisting many other life forms
and energies.

Karma is our path of learning and growing, the belief is that
what you do in this life affects you in this life or your next life,
we also call it law and effect, what you give out you get back
ten-fold or three-fold if your Pagan or a witch. So if you are
cruel and mean then it comes back on you. If you are kind and
caring it also comes back in a positive way. Let's face it we
have all done things we regretted, or wish we had behaved
differently. However, there are all those lessons and growth to
consider too.
I have found most of those people that love and care, act this
way without thought of reward, it is simply a genuine
unconditional love that reaches out naturally, look for a reward
for a kind deed and it will back fire.
We are also aware, and it has been proved by science, our
physical body, has a vibrational frequency, every ones
vibrational frequency is unique to them, just as their
fingerprint, no two are alike.

We are in fact multi-dimensional beings, shimmering and flickering and a mass of, beautiful colours like lights. With a central spark of divine light; like a shining star.

When the physical body dies, what remains is the vibrational frequency along with a glow of shimmering light with conscious mind energy, it can be classed as the soul, this is what remains, and returns to the source.
You may be reborn once more at a later date to learn more lessons, or you may already come from a higher rung of the Astral Ladder and return here to help once more.
These higher beings that return take on many forms they don't walk around with a sticker on their heads saying, 'Hi I'm a reincarnated Wise One, Star Person or Angel etc, they tend to keep a low profile, but some are clear for all to see such as Avatars, like Mother Meera, or the late Sia Baba, and many others, and because they take on human form they can also be subject to the ills and problems we also suffer, and yet they spread their wisdom and light amongst mankind and Mother Earth.

Buddhists believe we are reincarnated many, many times until we reach enlightenment, or Nirvana.
Some cultures believe we can be reincarnated into animals and insects, some wearing covers over their mouths to prevent swallowing flies, just imagine swallowing Aunty Flo she'd have something to say next time around, I jest!
There is lots of scope for exploration, as most religions and belief systems believe in some form of after life, and have names for their gods and goddesses. And if you study religion's beliefs you will see they all have a main core theme flowing through them, just given different names for the same thing and worshiped in a different way, and also man's personal interjection and interpretation in there too.

For me personally, God is a universal conscious energy, full of love and light, I do not believe he/she is of gender or that he/she smites and punishes us for our sins.

I know from experience when some of the soul rescues have been from lower astral realms that they too can have a chance to move to the light.

Whether you believe in any form of God energy or not, the source of light does not instantly forgive the reprobate who has done something very bad, unless he/she is truly sorry, for what they have done, it isn't just forgive and forget, and you are on your way to whatever you believe waits for us when this earth walk is over, Those that have committed terrible acts, They too, as I said earlier they are taken aside and worked with by special beings. They may even have to reincarnate a number of times.

You may now be wondering why we can't remember our past lives, as I mentioned earlier in general, the old soul stays within the newborn child for six weeks and then forgets, with the exceptions of the newborn advanced souls.

If all souls remembered, it might influence their work and lessons that they may be here to learn in this life.

We normally work out when following a spiritual path, that we have had some sort of past life that is affecting this life, feelings, memories and fears but to name a few things trigger our senses. It's like a big jigsaw piece by piece fits into place and can answer many questions.

A few of my reincarnations

From an early age I feared water wheels, and dark water I could not see the bottom of. It came to my knowledge that I had been executed as a witch in a past life. I was tied to the water wheel, my back was broken, and I eventually drowned.

My past lives have included a Wise Woman, in the time of Boudicca, Egyptian priestess, an Edwardian, Native Indian, and a lady in the fifteen century, a small child in the holocaust, a servant in Aztec times, and others that I can't recall at this time, most ended in a messy death.

In five of my past lives I have been involved with the same people, who are present in this life time, four of which were the hands that led to my deaths.

One day a client came to me for the second time, I finished my treatment and she rested in her out of body state, as I waited for her to return, I too began to drift into an altered consciousness, I recognised her from a past life, and memories came flooding back, it was a strange feeling. We became very close friends, and further regressions over the years showed we have had a number of lifetimes together.

You will find you have what is called a soul group and as you learn and grow you will find you have strong connections, with some people.

You may find someone who was the person that instigated one of your deaths, please don't hold it against them, you will probably find you may have in fact, caused their death too as I had in a previous life. I was very upset at the time, knowing that I had hurt her even though it was a hundreds of years ago. And yet it didn't bother me that she had been the cause of my death. It is a very strange and extensive topic the world of reincarnation.

Not all regressions have such a gloomy ending, and on occasions I have had people with no past life memories at all, they do seem to be very innocent in their outlook and child-like in a lovely way. Some we have identified that it is their first time on this plain.

In some regressions the individual is quite disappointed to find they had a very normal life and died of old age, or they come out with a smile on their face, as they have had the most wonderful life.

I did have one niggling thought which had been with me all my life and it is only in the last three years, that I understood why I had this feeling.

In the early days before my spiritual path had opened, I had the deep feeling that I didn't belong here, it feels like I am waiting for the mother-ship to take me home, I also have the classic light behind the eyes on occasions, which indicates star person origin.

Many years ago when I was at 'Highfields' with my foot in each world battles going on, I kept asking Spirit, 'What am I' One day they must have been getting a bit fed up with my constant questioning, and self-doubting, and a voice shouted back at high volume, 'Star Child.'!!!!!

Quickly followed my next question to spirit; 'What's one of them?' In my heart I already knew the answer. And everything was shown to me some years later.

There is a book by Doreen Virtue, called 'Earth Angels', it is well set out and easy to follow, she explains the different types of incarnations, now at the time of writing, and there are others too which are not in the book, but it may give you some inclination to your feelings of origin.

I'm a bit of a mixed bag, and have traits from several, so goodness knows where I have been and what I got up to, however I consider myself truly lucky.

Recent work has shown me my source origins and where I will return to when my time comes. It is quite a comforting feeling, and yet when you're feeling low or going through a bad patch it gives feelings of been homesick.

I always believed and felt I was sent here for a reason, even as a child, knowing I was different to the other children and that I was here to do something, at the time I couldn't explain or

really understand why, it was just this deep gut feeling in
the pit of the stomach that wouldn't go away.
Now I know why, I wished on occasions I had known earlier,
why I am here and where I came from. On the other hand there
were life lessons to learn, and one pattern I repeated over and
over again until I learned.
Then my life began to run with spiritual path my destiny some
of which I believe is why I am here.
I sometimes wonder if there were moments when spirit sat on
their clouds almost pulling their hair out at my stubborn and
self-doubting nature, and I know I've messed their plans up on
a number of occasions. I will share one such instance with you.
I knew about an event which would take place and affect me
personally, at first I accepted it, and took it on the chin, and
then my own insecurities got the better of me.
I was told 'To leave it and not interfere' the voice of my friend
in spirit David, rang in my ears as I walked up the stairs
shaking with nerves, I ignored him even though the voice and
the vision of him was so clear, jumping in with both feet, like
a mad March hare. He said, 'Leave it alone it's not time yet'
I don't' know how many times he repeated it following me up
the stairs and yet I still waded in well over my wellingtons and
up to my neck as a result. I caused myself more problems, and
I in fact changed my own future and made things much more
difficult for myself.

Looking into our past lives can be done with a regression
meditation, it is not difficult to do, but great care must be
taken, as you are opening up the mind of an individual into the
past. And you don't know what they will find or how it will
affect them mentally and physically.
I personally will not regress, someone unless I'm sure of their
stability and mental state or I feel it may be of benefit to that
person, to help with issues or problems they may have. I won't

do it for curiosities sake. I will often ask to meet a person a number of times before carrying out the process.

If you do decide to have a regression please do make sure they are recommended and practicing safely. You are accessing past life memories, and you must consider if you are able to handle an unpleasant death or some other incident, should it occur. Reincarnation and regression is a topic that once again is vast, and can lead to all sorts of experiences good and bad. It can answer questions, or leave you with more. Sometimes regression happens naturally within mediation or journeying with spirit.

It's not something that you should play with like scrying, take it seriously and remember like hypnosis it accesses the brain and deep memories.

There are rules with regression.

- Make sure the person who regresses you is well able and practices safely
- That you feel comfortable and trust the person
- Make sure you are of stable/sound mind,
- Don't do it if you are upset, angry
- Or suffering from any mental health condition, be it depression, anxiety, stress etc.
- Do not practice while under the influence of drugs or alcohol.
- Make sure you will not be disturbed for the duration of the session.

Remember it is the past and can only serve as a lesson to remind you of how far you have come.

A very brief look at Auras and Chakras

So, we have looked at a little of my life and how I come to be writing the first part of my journey, the world of Spirit, Soul Rescuers, the Astral Ladder, and the wide range of beings of light that live there. You now know you are a multi-dimensional being, with a divine spark of light within you, that you may have had many life times, you have Karma to work through, life's lessons, a whole world running parallel with yours ,which has many dimensions.

You also house two very important things here on the earth plain in your physical life, you're aura, and your chakras, which are energy centers in our body, which we need to survive.

We have our physical body, flesh, blood and bone and everything else that goes with it, how complex is this physical body alone, we need to feed this amazing shell, for this we need food, water, heat, shelter, warmth, and light.

Our Aura and Chakras need another form of energy that works in harmony with our physical body, they too need a food source in order to thrive, these are day light and the colours, with in the light spectrum, and we also need the vibrational energies, which come from the universal source, form Mother Earth and other energy life forms. You are well aware of how your body works and what it needs on the physical level, but on the ethereal level your need is very different.

Therefore we will start with sunlight, the sun rises and it sets, as it has done for thousands of years, we take it for granted it sees us born into the world and it sees us leave it. Without sunlight we will die, not just because the plant life can't grow, and there would be no oxygen to support life.

We also need the full colour spectrum within sunlight, to keep us healthy.

A few facts you need to know,

- light is made up of the colours of the rainbow,
- Each colour has a wave length and a vibrational frequency.
- Those with a higher vibration and shorter wave length generate more power. For example violet which is a very high powered colour used in healing and it is also the colour of Reiki energy.
- Violet is also found in X-Rays.
- At the other end of the scale we have red, which has a lower vibrational frequency and a longer wave length. Red is the colour of microwaves which are use, for example a microwave oven.
- We are often taught there are seven colours of the rainbow, although there are many more colours, far more than our eyes can detect.
- There are in fact over ten million different colours we are able to see, and who knows how many there are beyond our vision.
- It is also only primates who have a good colour vision like us, cats and dogs see three to four colours, insects two. So buying cuddles the cat a pink bed because you think she will like the colour, forget cuddles buy it because you like it.
- When you do a colour healing mediation like in the first steps exercise on page, you instinctively, know what colour your body, and mind needs to heal and balance.

Colour Exercise,

Let's work with an awareness exercise, it is very simple and will give you an idea of number of colours there are in just a small space,

- ❖ First look at an area about a foot square near you, it can be floor, ceiling, wall, or an item near you, anything that's comfortable to view.
- ❖ Now focus on this area
- ❖ What colours can you see?
- ❖ Stay with this area in your vision, look even more closely
- ❖ How many different shades of colour,
- ❖ How many different flecks of colours,
- ❖ If there's a pattern how many shades and flecks with in the main body of colour
- ❖ In different light there will be a different range of colours. .

Surprised at what you see? The more you practice this exercise the more in-depth your view and understanding of the world of colour is, you become so aware that the world around you takes on a new vision, like someone gave you some special glasses that helps you to see more clearly, and you begin to see the world around you in a different light literally, it's like you have never really seen colour before.

Excises like this also work in a spiritual growth way too by helping you to increase your awareness and perception; these are a part of the psychic development path.

When we are in the sunlight we are exposed to the full spectrum of colours that our body needs for health, unfortunately due to the damage in our atmosphere the sunlight

can also be dangerous. So do follow safety guidelines when you are out in the sunlight.
This is a brief explanation of how our body responds to the sun light; once again it is colour therapy. It is a vast subject as sound is also coloured this who topic has its feet firmly in quantum physics.

- ❖ When the spectrum of light hits our skin the nerves beneath respond,
- ❖ They intern send a message to the brain, telling it about the quantity of sun light we have received,
- ❖ This affects the endocrine system,
- ❖ First the brain tells the hypothalamus, this is our body clock; it tells use when to sleep, eat controls temperature etc,
- ❖ The hypothalamus then influences the pineal and pituitary gland.
- ❖ These glands also influence the thyroid, thymus, pancreas, gonads/ ovaries and adrenals.
- ❖ The pineal and pituitary gland take the process a step further, they detect the quality and quantity of light and also the vibrational frequencies and the wave lengths of the colours with in the light we have received via our nerve endings in our skin.
- ❖ The colour is broken down into vibrational frequencies and vibrations frequency's then become a source of energy.
- ❖ This energy, travels through energy points and lines called meridians, these same points are used in acupuncture, pressure point massage, reflexology therapy, sonic sound puncture plus many more,
- ❖ This energy feeds the Chakras within the body.

This is not the end of the process,

The energy that has now been broken down into frequencies and vibrations now moves in to the Chakras. The chakras are like wheels and turn creating a type of vortex, if you imagine the tips of two funnels end to end this will give you an idea what they look like.

* ❖ There are seven major chakras, and many others but we will remain with the seven for now.
* ❖ They are situated down the center of the body over the endocrine system which is listed above
* ❖ Like the funnels end to end with the narrowest point in the center of your body, where the chakra is located
* ❖ The front funnel shape openings of these Chakras are known as the feeling centers
* ❖ The back openings of your chakras are known as the will centers.
* ❖ All the energy from the chakras goes through the meridians and feeds the endocrine system and the body's organs, beneath the relevant chakra area.

Chakras are incredibly complicated and affect every part of our wellbeing, mentally, emotionally physical and spiritual, they have been known about for thousands of years and also have Sanskrit names, the following is a very brief introduction to give you some idea on how important they are.

The first chakra or base chakra
This chakra is situated low over the pelvic bone, it is the colour red. – Red relates to adrenals, kidneys, and the spinal column. Mentally it is connected to issues like keeping us more earthed, stable and grounded, as the saying goes feet firmly on the ground, when balanced it keeps your mind focused on your survival needs and also on physical health and creativity.

The second chakra or sacral chakra

Is situated about three finger widths below the belly button, and it is orange in colour. - The colour orange is linked to the gonads/ovaries, and reproductive areas. Mentally it links to Emotional, sensuality, sexuality and desires, it controls relationships and interactions with others its connects us to our family members, it is linked to self-respect, giving yourselves freedom to be yourself, respecting your own boundaries, and respecting others boundaries

The third chakra solar plexus

It is situated at the base of the sternum, and linked to the stomach liver and gall bladder, it is yellow in colour.
Yellow signifies the battery/power pack for the physical body. This is also the energy point used in martial arts; mentally it is related to how we view others and how we view ourselves in areas of personality, ego and intellect

The fourth chakra or heart chakra

Situated the Centre of the chest and over the heart, linked to thymus, heart, blood, and circulatory system it is green ad sometimes flecked with pink it is also the bridge between the physical and spiritual plain. Mentally it is linked to Love and in controls unconditional feelings and thoughts, relations and compassion, self-love, and relates to nurturing ourselves.

The fifth chakra or throat chakra–

This is linked to thyroid, bronchial, lungs, vocal, and alimentary canal. It is a turquoise blue in colour. Mentally it is linked to self-expression, to communicate needs, spirit of truth and purpose, linking communication with this world and the next

The sixth chakra or third eye chakra
Is situated over the forehead, and has many names, it is the seat of intuition and is indigo in colour, Linked to the pituitary, lower brain, left eye, ears and nose, This is the area that opens up when we link with the spiritual world, plus it is the focal point for spiritual development an higher awareness and growth of mind energy, mentally encouraging us to be responsible for our own life's, to follow the souls path, and trusting your intuition looking at things from a higher perspective, the intuition and feelings from the brow chakra feel very different from gut feelings.

The seventh chakra or crown chakra
This chakra is a direct connecter to source energy whatever you believe it to be, it is white, but can be seen in a number of shimmering opalescent shades of colour, often a golden light or violet light are also seen. It is linked to the pineal gland and the upper brain and the right eye. Mentally it is linked to self-awareness, self-knowledge and spiritual awareness, union with higher self and higher consciousness.

There are other higher chakras but at this stage these are the ones to concentrate on until you are more developed, also they have colours that are used to balance and heal them, the same can be said of the aura it too directly affects us mentally, physically, and spiritually. This is a brief introduction to the world of chakras; there are many other aspects that relate to them, and many ways of bringing healing and balance to all areas of your life an in-depth look at chakras and auras is in my next book 'Release your phoenix'
So we will just have a quick summary of the above.

- ❖ We have seven Chakras down the Centre of our body working our way up from red, orange, yellow, green, blue, indigo, white/golden, other colours in higher chakras can be seen.
- ❖ Each of these Chakras, are situated over the seven sets of major organs, and glands.
- ❖ As the Chakras rotate they absorb the colour frequencies and wave lengths,
- ❖ Turning it in to a source of vibrational energy our bodies can use.
- ❖ This energy then travels through meridian lines, and through other small chakras carrying the energy to all areas of the body.

The Lack of Light

When we do not receive good quality light or not enough natural light the chakras can't function correctly, and this causes them to rotate too fast or become sluggish, this is when dis-ease slips in, and ill health will start.

You may well think that artificial light would be a good substitute, however that is not the case, artificial light does not give the full colour spectrum, and although better than nothing over time ill health will follow.

Chakras and auras can be balanced by a wide range of energy healing methods such as Reiki, spiritual healing, reflexology, sound vibrations, colour therapy, crystals and many holistic and therapeutic practices; it is easy to apply healing yourself.

Colour therapy, crystals and the use of colour in general, is a very easy and simple way to energize any Chakra that is out of balance.

Here are just two simple ways:-.

❖ Place a piece of colored acetate sheet or paper around a glass of water, cover and leave it in the sunlight. The vibrations of the colour will permeate the water, and when drunk, aid the individual.

❖ Colour therapy is easy to use in day to day life wearing colours, is simple to do, also your body knows what colours it needs to balance itself. It can be anything a scarf, skirt, dress or tee-shirt etc, anything you have in your wardrobe really.
So if that jumper Aunty Flo knitted you feels good wear it.

We have a lot to thank the Egyptians and ancient civilization's for, they practiced reflexology, massage and used aromatherapy, but to name a few therapies. They used colour to heal over four thousand years ago, which they applied by placing the person in a stone building with openings in which they positioned gem stones, sunlight reflected through the gems amplifying the colours and shining on to the person, thus giving healing to the patient.

They too knew about the Auras and Chakras. They also knew the body was not just made of physical matter

And so we will now have a brief look at the Aura.

The Aura

The Aura is linked to light too, it is made up of seven layers,
note there are seven colours of the rainbow, and seven Chakras,
and each layer of the aura, connects to each Chakra.
Each Chakra connects to a gland and each gland connects to
the organs.
It is like the old song. The toe bones connected to the foot
bone, the foot bones connected to the ankle bones, and so on.
Just be glad you can't hear me singing!!!

- ❖ The Aura is a field of pulsating and vibrating energy,
- ❖ It can span from several inches to a few feet wide,
- ❖ It fluctuates in thickness and colour throughout the
  day.
- ❖ It can become like a wall, or spiky, and create a barrier
  when we don't want someone near.
- ❖ If you are feeling over whelmed it can shrink, like you
  have been wrapped in cling film.
- ❖ It can become fuzzy if you haven't the strength or
  courage to keep some one away from you.
- ❖ It reflects our mental, physical, and spiritual well-
  being.
- ❖ Your aura will reach out and touch another person's
  Aura, if you like them or care about them, if you are in
  love the auric fields are intertwined.
- ❖ The aura is a cloud of energy constantly moving and
  undulating with the moods and feelings within us.

When a person is ill or stressed, I have found the aura to be
darker and shadowy in its energy or it may be close to the body
and the person may be experiencing a feeling of tightness, if a
person is unbalanced they may well find yourself stumbling or

been accident prone. Forthcoming illness or psychic attacks can be seen in the Aura. I view it often as a shadowy type of energy manifesting as a rip like in cloth or a convex or concave shape, even jagged in shape over time this damage will grow and becomes deeper until in penetrates the physical body bringing with it a range of issues and problems.

A method called Kerilian photography can be used to take a photograph of person's aura. The photo will reveal what is going on in their aura.

The aura appears around a person like a mist of different colours; Spirit can also be seen in an aura along with the person's mental, physical and spiritual states.

As I mentioned earlier the aura movies and changes with a person's moods, and becomes a wall or spiky, it is a natural reaction to place a barrier between us and someone else, for example, if we don't like them or we have had an argument.

Can you remember back to a time when you knew someone was angry at you, perhaps no words had been spoken, but you knew, you will automatically place a barrier or pull your Aura away from them it is an instinctive and naturel response you don't even think about it. And yet you can sense a person is angry or upset with you.

Sometimes a person can leave you feeling uncomfortable as an example; think back to a time when you have had someone bump into you while when you are out.

Did they make you feel repulsed or an unpleasant feeling?

Have you met people who spend time with you and when they have gone leave you feeling like you have been sucked dry or feel tired and lethargic,? Or in some cases feel energized?

This is because the aura is a field of energy, this can be drawn by another person, leaving you feeling drained. Sometimes people dump their negative feelings in your auric field you also find you feel low or depressed. This often happens when you are working in a helping capacity.

So you need to be able to recharge your auric energy, not from others but from the universal source, from light, mother earth, and also learn to channeled energy, and how to protect your auric energy field.

These things I will explain further later in the book.

The Layers of the Aura

As I mentioned there are seven auric layers, and they vary in colour and thickness and vibrations

- ❖ The first layer of the aura is close to your body. This is known as the Etheric Body, it is blueprint image of your physical self, and connects to the Base Chakra over the pelvic area. This Auric layer tends to be the colours of blue to grey.
- ❖ The second layer is called the Emotional Body and is connected to the Sacral Chakra; this layer varies in colour, from dark colours to clear and bright colours.
- ❖ The third layer is called the Mental Body and is connected to the Solar Plexus it tends to be bright yellow, the more a person is thinking the brighter it shines.
- ❖ The fourth layer is called the Astral Body; it is connected to the Heart Chakra and tends to be rose pink in colour.
- ❖ The fifth layer is called the Etheric Template, it is linked to the Throat Chakra and this links to all the other chakras, it is oval in shape, and looks like the negative of a photograph.
- ❖ The sixth layer is called the Celestial Body, this is the level of unconditional love, it is opalescent and glows

like a candle, it is also connected to the third eye or brow Chakra.
❖ The seventh layer is called Ketheric Template and connected to Crown Chakra and the colour gold.

The Chakras and Aura are one of the first things you need to learn about, this will open a large door to your development that will lead into the world of spiritual and psychic development.
The sensing of energy leads on to sensing the aura, this is a starting point that leads on to ability's like medium-ship,
We also need to work on protecting the aura, in the same way we protect ourselves from negative energy, as described earlier in the book, remember the section using, angels, prayer chant etc, and then you learn how to recharge the aura, in turn also recharging the chakras.
This following exercise is an easy and effective way to start; I have known people who didn't really believe in the world of energy, go on to rapid awareness and growth after sensing the energy available to us.

How To Feel Energy

Try this simple exercise.

❖ Rub your hands together,
❖ Then hold them about 10 inches' apart.
❖ Close your eyes and slowly bring your hands together,
❖ Bring your hands forward and back to each other, slowly.

In time if you keep practicing you will feel a resistance and a pulling sensation like two magnets pushing each other away, having your eyes closed makes sensing much easier.

The next step, as you become aware of energy:-

❖ Try placing your open hand with fingers closed and palms facing an animal or plant. Plants also have an energy field, and animals have chakras, if you feel confident try it with a friend.
❖ Start with hands to hands, palms facing each other, holding your palms away from them with eyes closed move you palm back and forth until you feel a resistance, this is the aura.
❖ If there are more than two of you practice with each other, stand in a circle palm to palm.
❖ It takes time to perfect these exercises, so be patient.

Once you are proficient in feeling energy, your field of energy and use of energy will increase and will never view things the same again, learning to see it becomes part of the process. But like anything it takes time and perseverance.

How to See the Aura

You can try this exercise in a number of ways,

❖ Sit in a room in front of mirror, in day light, but close the curtains so it is not too bright, if you have thick curtains that block out the light, a couple of small lamps in the back ground should be lit, but not behind or in front of you a side position is fine. A light overhead isn't recommended for viewing either;
❖ You need to be in front pale coloured wall, or hang a pale sheet up to make a background, behind you. This is a good way when there are a group of you learning to

see Auras. You don't need a lot of room just enough to see at least form your shoulders up over your head.

❖ Sit in front of your mirror and look about a two inches, above your head, focus on this area, If you are able defocus your eyes slightly.

❖ You will see a creamy white light around the top of your head this is the first layer of the Aura. The reason it is easier to see is because it contains physical matter like dust and skin particles.

❖ Over time some people go on to see auras and their colours. But mostly it is the sensing that is strongest.

Protecting the Aura

This is a very important area and the need to protect your aura is a general requirement as you evolve spiritually, especially if you go on to work in a professional capacity, and it's not always easy, visualization is very important as the saying goes, 'The thought is the deed.'

There are many methods and most are simple to use, but it doesn't last so you need to make a conscious effort to keep your protection topped up, adopt a protection method you feel comfortable with, fitting it into your life style like brushing your teeth, or having a shave.

In my early growth I had many unpleasant experiences of what happens when you do not protected your aura.

Most people just simply need to put up a shield of protection to stop their energy being taken by others, keeping energy vampires out, and stop their energy field leaking away.

Also to stop others from depositing their negative energies or entities, which detach themselves from one host and then transfer to another; this doesn't happen to everyone only a minority.

Here is one of my first experiences of an attachment coming into my aura unbeknown to me.

When I was living at `Highfeilds' in 1998, a friend named Rosie came to visit me and my Reiki Master and as I worked on her, we both sensed a great deal of unhappiness and disharmony and proceeded to give healing. When they had both left I was aware that Rosie had left someone with me, focusing on him, he said he was her nice grandfather William. I welcomed him and said little more.

That night, I felt very unsettled, and as the night went on it became much worse, I slept badly, eventually not going to sleep, and I gave up and got out of bed very early the next morning. The urge to be out in the sunlight was very strong, so with hast I dressed and went into the garden,

It was a fresh morning, a sharp crisp wind bit into my face slapping any exposed parts of flesh, I pottered around the garden feeling very unsettled but still couldn't understand why. As I tried to rake up leaves, the wind blew and the task was never ending and yet the need to persist in my job wouldn't leave me although I knew it was pointless. As I was focusing on my leaves, out of the blue Rosie appeared briskly approaching me up my drive towards me. I was surprised to see her, 'Hello.' she said.

Before I had even formed my words, I felt as if a large strip of sticky paper had been ripped forcibly off my front, with such a force I thought I was going to be pulled over.

I breathed in fresh air and filled my lungs and as I did this I began to feel instantly better. I later learnt that Rosie had a nice granddad and a nasty granddad. It would seem that the nasty one had attached to me and the nice one hung around. We discovered this was part of Rosie's problem, and over the years the nasty one was removed.

Had I known than about the importance of protecting myself, possibly he might not have been able to attach himself to me. Remember do not make yourself vulnerable to the invisible. And remember you don't always see what is coming save yourself some disharmony, use protection.

Ways of Protecting Your Auric Field

Please remember there are many ways of protecting yourself, whether it is in daily life, or when working with energies and Spirit. Your method of protecting yourself will change as you grow and develop, no persons way of protecting themselves is wrong, it is personal to you the individual. Like your fingerprint or, the vibration frequency of your Aura, it is as individual as you are unique.

There is a list of ways to protect yourself, on page 120 and 121

I use different methods depending on what is affecting me, I do have armor when I am fighting lower astral dwellers', and the blue light for protection when I'm being targeted by negative forces as I develop other methods were also channeled in for me to use. A new one which came in 2008 is a vast fire like field which radiated out with force and pushes whatever is bothering me away; it is connected to source, for protection around others. This fire like energy appears as a phoenix. And the phoenix has popped up ever since I started to write the draft of my book all those years ago. Hear as I finish this book at last, many other forms of energy and protection have been taught to me.
And remember if all else fails and your struggling no matter how advanced you are please, call on your fellow spiritual colleagues to help, we are all in this together. In some cases

we need to join our energies in order to be strong, or remove and deter some negative forces.

A Brief Look at Negative Entities & Energy Vampires

There are many negative influences in the world, whether it's caused by mankind's own doing, or from external forces. The negative energy I'm briefly going to talk to you about comes from within the realms of the Spirit world. Have no doubt negative or evil forces if you wish to call them, are at work on the various plains of existence.

Just as most religions point out good versus evil, many of us believe that there has to be a balance of good and evil, or negative and positive vibrations as I prefer to call it.

It doesn't matter what name you use, over many decades, negative has been gaining the upper hand, and the scales have tipped in its favor. The result being, a new age of people have evolved to serve the light to readdress the balance, so one day in the future positive light forces will be in control.

Energies from the negative side come in all shapes and sizes, and varying degrees of abilities. During the early part of my growth many of the negatives came from people, dead and alive draining me.

They tend to choose the moments when we are at our lowest ebb; feeling ill, depressed, or at times in your life when things are not going well. It is often at those times when negative energies slip in unnoticed. Sometimes they are as bold as brass, they will openly challenge, or try to find a chink in your armor. Ask yourself what your vulnerable point is, it may be physical or a mental one.

It may be something no one in your life knows about but you, something deep and personal. They know when it is a good time to nobble you, remember though like I said, before you need to find balance, not all events in your life are caused by you being 'nobbled,' as we call it some are just life's rich tapestry of events, and experiences. Look at the logical first.

For those using negative spells, or wishing harm on others, it will come back to the sender tenfold or threefold, whichever law you believe in, as I have said before you reap what you sow, whether in this life or the next.

It is very hard sometimes to forgive those that hurt you, if you do manage to forgive the burden is lighter to bear, and forgiving someone does not mean you condone their actions against you.

In the Louise Hay books there are lessons on how to cut the energy ties that connect you, to people you no longer wish to be connected with. And how your physical health can manifest itself from an emotional source, there are a number of her books and others that will help you in your daily life.

You will find the shops are full of spell books, to tell you how to cast a spell for the desired outcome, most people are quite capable of making a spell work, as the saying goes, 'The thought is the deed' It is not difficult to do whether in fun or in seriousness.

If you cast a spell to get something you desire whether it be love or fortune, if it is not meant to be truly yours you will not keep it, and it may cause you more heartache in the long run. If there is something you desire ask the world of Spirit and always add on the end, 'If it is for my highest good' this way, if it is not for your highest good then you will not sabotage your own path. Trust in the law of supply and demand; what is needed will come to you when appropriate.

Affirmations are a more positive way to acquire what you need, whether it is good health or some other item your heart desires.

An affirmation is a phrase repeated over and over again, for example health, 'Every day in every way I get better and better and better' it is especially good to say an affirmation at night, just before you got to sleep, it will soak into your sub–conscious.

You could say something like – 'I accept with a grateful heart the gifts that the universal force wishes to give me' There are many affirmations plus ways of working with issues that hold you back in your life.

A good place to start would be with Louise Hay books, these self-help books work in a holistic and spiritual way to bring about practical changes to help you heal issues in your life and reach out to help you achieve your full potential.

Well earlier I promised you some good old fashioned ghost stories, and looking through the box of notes and diaries this folder is fatter than any other, not because I remember them more than any other spiritual happening. Mostly the reason is because there has been so many, and at the end of the day it is my job and part of what I came back here to do. I have considered carefully the affects that my stories might have on you the reader. I don't want to unnerve or alarm you in any way so I have carefully chosen a few stories that I will recount to you. I will reserve juicier stories for my book – ` Phoenix in the Shadows.'

Remember most people do not have Spirit attachments.

I made the choice to work with the dead, in a number of ways, and you may wish to work with energy and not Spirit. That's fine if you operate by free will, what you work with is your choice. My faith and belief can have no spark of doubt within it or I would be done for.

I think a good place to start is with negative energies, those you are most likely to come across on your spiritual path, and they can attempt to hamper your growth and development.

One of the first negative types of energy I became aware of was those energies left by death and trauma; followed by energies left in my aura by people who were in and out of my life, some for moments, and others for longer. The effects they had on me varied from being violently sick to taking on their emotions, pain, to various feelings of exhaustion and fatigue.

Just a Few Examples of Negative Attachments

Summer 1999 – A lady came to me for a back massage, and Reiki, within moments she fell asleep, and during healing I was told she would have a healing crisis. When I had finished the treatment, she sat up, and looking directly into my eyes, her blue eyes had turned as black as coal, and I must admit although I knew what was happening I was still a little unnerved.

She had a Spirit attachment within her, who was none too pleased, the treatment had altered her auras vibration and it could no longer remain in its host. Over the next three days she was violently ill and very weak.

When I saw her a week later she had a spring in her step and looked lively. Until treating her she had been very low and also very subservient to her dominating husband, she had changed in far more ways than just her liveliness, she wasn't afraid to challenge his behavior towards her, and she had become stronger and more self-assured in nature.

Whilst I was training in 2000 I was in contact with a young woman, who had some very unusual energy.

In the middle of the boiling summer heat she would come in wrapped up in winter woolies, and proceeded to close all windows; whilst the rest of us melted in the heat, like a chocolate bar on a car seat. I am aware now that her illness was one of her mind, a fear of being ill made her very anxious, and in turn she felt ill.

She was an unusual girl, with grey, clammy looking skin,
and piercing eyes which seemed to bore into your very being
making you feel that you did not want to look at her.
Class was always disrupted when she was there, for one reason
or another normally an incident that she would be the instigator
of, this in turn gained her the desired attention she wanted.
Due to this the class was disbanded and I was the only student
refusing point blank to give up my training, even though my
tutor reminded me just how much I didn't like feet. (It was a
reflexology course, you see). The stubborn nature of the `Aries,
'part of me was brought into force and I refused to let it go; as I
had signed up for an aromatherapy class at the same time as the
reflexology,
I came across her again in a new class, it seemed she was a
well know individual, by many locals, a pattern of arguments
ensued. That familiar uneasy feeling filtered through to the
other students. No one wanted to work with her and this
resulted even in one student locking herself firmly in the toilet
refusing to come out. So I took on the role of rescuer and
agreed to work with her, Whilst I gave her treatments it was
fine, and had no ill effect, the reverse can be said when she
gave treatment to me it was very difficult to keep her out of my
Aura. It was like something nasty trying to work its way in
like a venomous snake. Another student that was familiar with
the girl had offered to give me Reiki after I had worked with
her, I refused at the time. I knew I had picked up a Spirit
attachment. However, I wasn't sure what kind of attachment
and I didn't want to put her at risk. I left college heading home
feeling sick, cold and shaking, sensations like I had been
violated, in some way.
On the way home the Spirit of a man made himself known. He
told me he was angry with the girl, she had caused him great
pain and it was not healing. He tried so hard but she would not
listen. I felt his pain, anger and frustration, who he was he

never said, I knew by his emotions the girl was obviously important to him. He was also very exhausted with all his efforts, I suggested he took time out to recharge his batteries, within the world of Spirit and perhaps someone else could help her for a time.

Still cold and shaking, the urgency to have a bath was strong as washing something dirty from my body, and I made this my first priority, looking forward to my long peaceful soak.

I ran the bath, placing my hand expectantly into the warm water, to my surprise the water was stone cold.

I ran the bath again, and once more the water was cold, so logically I checked the boiler everything was working fine. Eventually I ran the third bath, and yes the water was freezing cold, although the water in the kitchen was warm there was no storage tank it was a direct supply system, and on the opposite side of the wall to the bath reluctantly I knew a cold bath was on the cards for a reason and so braving its icy ripples, I had my cold bath, needless to say a very, very quick one, rushing off to the snug effect of my warm bed.

First thing the following morning I ran the boiler repair man, and later that day, I check the boiler again. Then I cancelled the appointment, as I realised that there was nothing wrong with the boiler. I later understood that a cold bath was needed to clean the negative energy from my aura, another chilling lesson of a different kind.

Summer 2001- A lady rang me -
'I need an appointment' she spluttered
'What treatment would you like' I replied
'Anything, I need something,' her desperation was obvious in her voice and I arranged for her to come at seven o'clock that evening. So we could look at her situation and form a treatment plan.

She arrived bang on seven o'clock, a weary looking lady, stressed to the hilt and not knowing what she needed.

I had been told by Spirit to put on the Selfic disk on before she came, I argued with them, 'If I do I can't give out healing,' at that time I could not heal when I wore it.

She talked for about forty five minutes, I was aware of the Spirit of her father stood by her; I relayed the fact he was there and gave her a message.

She spoke incessantly and to this day I don't remember much of the conversation, my head began to spin, sickness welled up in my stomach, then my head started to pound with a migraine, I managed to bring the session to a close some half hour later, I had attempted to earth myself and put up a stronger energy barrier, but it was too late the damage was done.

Trying not to allow my feelings known, I saw her out, she left, full of bounce and life, a very different woman to the previous hour. After she left I immediately took myself into the toilet and was I was violently ill, with a migraine. I spent the rest of the evening and next day in bed.

A lesson learned she had left all her negative rubbish behind; I had picked it up and processed the negative energy for her. I never saw her again although I rang her and tried to find her as she also borrowed some of my books. It was as though she didn't exist and yet she was only four streets away.

Whatever took place was meant to be. I had learned my lesson. I hope she found a new path and solution to her troubles.

Picking up negative and processing for others was something I naturally did in my quest to help others, it is not advisable. Years later I have learnt to help, but I made sure I was able to be in control so I wasn't ill afterwards.

On occasions I am asked to indeed process energy's and emotions for others, in a bid to help them move forwards, and yes it can make me unwell, and in the earlier days, I found there is normally a lesson within the experience and also I have agreed to help spirit with whatever they request and so for me if shouldering some discomfort can help a person move in the right direction then so be it. However, it is at spirits discretion and not my own, and I'm normally forewarned. Negative energy vibrations can be left by passing events from something as simple as an argument, to wars and battles of bye gone times, fallen warriors and war plane crash sites are often reported to have ghostly apparitions, these vibrations are not negative most are not classed as lower astral dwellers . They are victims of these particular tragedies, and have suffered enough, like a video tape they relive that fateful night over and over again. These people need help to find their way home to the light.

There are also other negative energies that are classed as demonic, who are nearer the source of evil, or lower down the Astral Ladder. If you are of Christian, Jehovah's Witness, Catholic faith etc., you may think of it as the devil, the boss of negative energy, the names are numerous.
They are in fact very low astral dwellers and are few and far between, in their visiting apparition forms they are more likely to come in a form that you would be afraid of or even trust, and so you need to call angels or beings of light to you a being of light will not dissipate when you say the lord's prayer or the equivalent.
I have no wish to scare or unnerve you, so for this book things will be kept light, remember these are rare cases.
The following one I will share with you is not about a demon, it is about some vampires. Sadly no sexy men or ladies, no dark capes, or white pointy fangs, no flying through the air and draining of blood, no pretty girls whisked of under the moon lit sky by the wicked Count, who will be slain by some professor, whose been chasing him half his life time, and will assist his exit from this world, with the aid, of a crucifix and a stake

through the heart, pure water, or proceed to have his
severed head prepared like a roast Sunday joint stuffed with all
the garlic the local super store can sell, or alas, the rise of the
morning sun.
Sorry dear readers these vampires don't seek blood, but energy
that precious field of vibrational frequencies that surrounds you
and flows through you, and keeps you in good health, Your
Aura.

This case took place in Africa with a very special lady called
Vera she had an air about her as if she was queen like, and in
past lives, she had in fact been just that in biblical times.
Vera, was a trance medium, she joined the Nottingham healing
group on very rare occasions as she was so busy working for
the light. She often had to take trips away, and respond to
requests for assistance at a minute notice, to calls of help from
others, sometimes taking her abroad; this particular case took
her back to Africa.
When she arrived at her destination, she met with the villagers
that had suspected something was not as it should be within the
village, they told her of their suspicions and fears, Vera went to
work, she soon noticed that things were not as they should be,
the villagers were ill and weak many died, and there was so
much suffering. However, the elder of the village, and his
close associates' were strong and well. Although he was of a
ripe old age he looked much younger than his years and he was
very fit and active.
This wasn't a case of him just being lucky enough to be that
way or because he was working for the light.
He had a way of creating good health and vitality, as he was
draining the village people of their life force energy; anyone
that he drew close to him took on the same good health and
vitally as him.

Vera set up a prayer house with a small number of
villagers, and worked with the universal light day and night to
stop his negative energies affecting the villages.

 Her husband described how he could see the demonic entities
running on the roofs of houses trying to get in but they could
not. The vampire elder's grip on the villages was broken after
many days of prayers and work. He could no longer feed on
them, over time he then became weak as the villagers' health
and lives improved then things returned to normal in the village
and it flourished.

And so these are just a few of the cases I have come across of
which there are so many. If your Aura is being drained then
your physical body feels it too. Can you recall meeting
someone who made you feel alive, or made you feel so
exhausted, and even ill. How many times has someone bumped
into you while say you are out shopping, nudging your arm or
shoulder as the passed and made you feel quite uncomfortable,
this is because as I have explained we are surrounded by the
Aura, an electromagnetic energy field, when someone is near
to us they can draw on our energy. Or in fact give us some of
theirs, or dump their negativity into our Aura. Leaving us to
deal with it, in an ideal situation if each individual is connected
to the universal source, whether they call it god or by another
name, they would not have an effect on others.

Some people do not connect to the source and never will even
when they have been told how to, and draw energy and from
the living. Most of these people do not do it intentionally,
some people you know will always feel doom and gloom, even
if something good enters their lives, these people can generate
a negative Aura and in fact attract negative energy to them
which makes their situation worse. Remember think positive
and you will attract positive into your life, even if the chips are
down and the odds stacked against you, think negative and you
are sure of a negative result. Those that draw on your energy

are not always aware and most like the lady in my earlier story. It is innocent and they don't know on a conscious level what they are doing, protecting and shielding yourself will prevent this happening.

There is another influence that is very important in our lives, and the energy balance of our planet, are the other planets, they affect us in so many ways with their vibrational energies, and one we all are aware of is the moon, as you know it controls, the seas and tides. Did you know? Our bodies are more than 70% water and therefore the planets have an effect on the human body in a range of ways.

The moon has the ability to affect some individuals moods, the old horror stories in the movies always have a moon hanging in there in the scene somewhere, as the thirsty vampire who is fond of a neck or two, swoops in for its prey or the werewolves finding their way to London that make its own takeaway meal out of some unsuspecting passer by walking his dog, not surprisingly some people become afraid of the dark.

On a full moon I myself become fully energised and feel very alive, there are other people who become violent, angry, tearful, or sensual.

My friend Billy, a strong man of God, doesn't believe in such things. A quiet non-drinking, no-smoking hard working man nevertheless when the moon was full he was a Dr Jeckyl turning into Mr Hide. He would be incredibly violent and aggressive. Another girl I knew called Sophia was kind and caring and yet the energies of the full moon also turned her violent and aggressive, and she often ended up in the police cells at the local station. The moon affects thousands of people in many different ways and some people are not affected at all The moon is not a negative influence but there are odd occasions when it can be,

One such occasion is the red moon, this came about in my
very early development when I had lived at 'Highfields' and I
had been with the Nottingham group for only a short while.
I will never forget, my experience with the red moon, it was
January 2001, while the world waited for the lunar eclipse to
take place, I was one of the exceptions, I had no idea there was
an eclipse due, I didn't read newspapers or watch much in the
way of TV or listen to the radio.
I was still in my early stages of growth and as I have
mentioned at this stage, I would experience an event and then
learn about what I had experienced afterwards, normally from a
book.
I had gone to work early that morning, and I hadn't felt quite
myself all day, by the time I set off home from work that
evening, I began to feel afraid, I became convinced my
children were in danger, I started to tremble and wanted to cry.
I tried to question myself logically, 'Why was I was feeling
like this?' 'Had something happened to the children?' My
daughter was fifteen and like all big siblings she would collect
her little brother from, the school bus feed him his first tea and
maybe his second tea, which is a habit he still has today and
has now become three or four, she would take care of him until
I returned home.
As I drove onto the drive, and started to walk up the drive,
Amy came out to greet me excited 'Look at the moon mum
there's an eclipse,' she pointed up to the clear night sky. I
looked up above my head, the sky was so clear, and the moon
just hung there like some beautiful orb of orange light. I
wondered how I could not have noticed it before. On entering
the house I put my Selfic disk on and aura soma through my
Aura, I still didn't feel right the children were safe. So what
was bothering me? The children seemed unaffected and carried
on with what they were doing. I went up to my bedroom, I felt
uneasy, and on edge, I sat in the chair and reached for the God

calling books, I chanted the lord's prayer, over and over
again calling in my Reiki guides, my head swam, I felt as if all
my senses were under attack, a Spirit presence appeared. The
left side of my head and face felt strange, logical thoughts
entered my head was I ill or something? I became aware that
the Spirit entity that was stood by me was trying to enter
without my consent, that familiar pressure when they come to
share with you before they slip into your Aura. I chanted more
and told it only light was welcome here and he could not enter
without my permission, it moved behind me and I felt its icy
touch like long fingers on my back, I knew he was trying to
enter at my psychic gate. I clutched at the Selfic disk and
continued to chant the prayer; I wanted to scream at the top of
my voice, I was so afraid, it felt as if I was fighting for my very
soul. How long I was like this I don't know, my son came
wandering in, 'Are you alright mummy?' He asked, I assured
him I was ok, and I would be down soon. I couldn't tell a six
year old I was under psychic attack from negative forces. I was
feeling very hot, my cheeks burnt and a dull headache pounded
its way through my brain, I felt exhausted, and drained, even
though the curtains were shut I could feel the eclipse was now
passing and I didn't have to look out at the night sky to see, I
knew. I pulled myself together and went downstairs to see to
the children putting them to bed and retiring myself. That night
I was afraid to sleep and chanted, and yet sleep was what was
needed, I lay on my bed in a semi-conscious daze, jumping to
my senses as a small dark figure appeared in a swirling black
mass of shapes a hand reaching out, I felt its hand pin my head
to the pillow, I was completely stuck fast, I instantly chanted
the lord's prayer for all I was worth, it released its grip and
vanished into the night.
I sat up in my bed and then climbed out pulling the curtains
back wide open, to reveal a clear and beautiful night sky
sprinkled with stars and a bright beautiful welcoming moon, its

rays reaching out like the caress of a lovers touch soothing, calming as if to say it's alright now, your safe, all is well. Hardly able to believe what had happened, I wondered had she too fought the negative energies which came to diminish her peaceful glow,

The following Wednesday I went to the Nottingham healing group, I waited wanting to ask them about what had happened hoping they would explain it all to me. As the group talked, Vera then breezed in and Wendy jumped to her feet,

'Can I put the Television on….., there's a bit about the red moon there's a ten minute program on about the red moon in India.'

My heart jumped with surprise and a sigh of relief, it wasn't just me that had felt its influence, Vera said she was exhausted and had been up all night praying to keep the negative energies away what kind they were she didn't say.

The program showed me that, in India the people gather by the River Ganges, the holy- men and wise men chant prayers throughout the night, the people turn all pots, pans, bowls, and vessels upside down anything that could catch falling rain, but it was not the rain they did not want to catch but the negative energies of the red moon.

Thousands of people from around the world prayed and chanted that night to counteract negative energy.

While many in the west slept unaware of the event that had taken place, some people in the western world think, third world countries are backwards, they may not have all the trapping of the western world, however they are more in tune with nature and all her workings. That western society's seems to have lost and is now trying to regain,

No amount of material wealth can compare, to the connection of earth and sky, it's priceless!

An Open Mind on Life and Death and God

Life and Death

And so as I approach the end of this book I am going to climb
on my soap box and waffle on about God, life and the universe.
To start with let us just have a light look at the big D word
which frightens some and is the wakeup call for others. It
comes to use all no matter who you are, it's one of the things
we all have in common. Death!!! Rich or poor, it won't matter
when the time comes; you can't take your material wealth with
you, where you are going you won't need it, besides they
would never get the coffin lid on. You can't escape it, no
amount of nip or tuck, hair dye, or even the freezing of your
body for future rejuvenation can prevent your soul from going
home.

That's what it's really all about going home, you are a multi-
dimensional being within a physical shell, your body is the
house for your soul or mind energy whatever you believe, how
you look after your shell, is up to you, and how long it lasts,
well that's a combination of how you take care of it and what
life throws at you.

We are up against chemicals, and pollution, additives to our
food and drink even the water from the taps has been through
more kidneys than you can imagine, research has shown that
although sewage is cleaned and put back into our rivers we
can't clean it of all traces, one result is that fish are not
reproducing as freely due to residues from the birth control pill
left in the water, so how many other things in our environment
affects us?

There is little we can do about some things but others like war,
inhumane acts, and our impact on the environment we can,
that's just the tip of the iceberg.

We have developed cravings for caffeine, chocolate and the rest, we convince ourselves that we need that chocolate bar or glass of coke, along with the T.V. adverts backing up our desires.

But hey! Have a heart, preferably a healthy one, despite all the things stacked against us we are making changes, and we are living longer, so we must be doing something right, even if it is because of all the preservative in our food, I joke !

We can all make small adjustments, imagine each individual doing just one thing to make a difference to aid our planet, see each individual as one piece of a jigsaw puzzle. Eventually as the pieces come together the jigsaw becomes bigger and the picture more complete despite it being so complex.

So where living longer and that brings with it the 'Age Landmarks' as we hit the big four 'o' suddenly men and women start thinking 'I'm half way or more through my life, what have I done with it?' 'What do I want?' And before you know it they are given the midlife crisis, tag. By those that are hurt by their actions, or praised by the friends who are in favor of the changes. You are told, 'Life begins at forty.' I must admit it wasn't far wrong for me; my life began at thirty eight. I have no regrets and never look back.

If you're thinking about what life's thrown at you, see the ups and downs as lessons, because that's why we are here.

Those experiences make you the person you are today, and the person you will be tomorrow or in the next life.

You can spend most of your life feeling sorry for yourself, worrying regretting, with comments, such as, 'I could have, I wish I had have, I had the opportunity to but ….' (we have a saying in counselling …everything before the but…. Is bull sh….t.) and for some people hating others, or unable to move forward.

There are the ones I feel most sorrow for; they only bind themselves to self-inflicted misery, making the rest of their lives unhappy.

You may feel some people deserve to suffer and why should they get away with it, they will one day have to atone for what they did, whether in this life or the next, Karma comes, so don't dwell on the past.

Take the bad experiences and turn them into new beginnings, it is better to face life with a thankful heart than grumbling lips.

Now where were we? Yes from the forties and onwards, as we question ourselves with comments such as, 'What, have I done with my life? thoughts.

We feel that we flit through the fifties and as we hit the sixties, many of us at this point feel we are nearing the front of the queue; we spend our time often talking about who died and what they died of, who doesn't look well and who will be next on the list to leave this mortal plain. We ask ourselves, 'Which bit hurts the most' and the doctor telling us it's to be expected at our age.

Shock as the people on television that you have watched all your life begin to die off one by one, and the love handles won't go away; middle age spread seems to have well, reached the middle in larger proportions.

The subject of death niggles, for many the mind is willing but the body weary from years of hard work. Think about those people, born before the second-world war, they left school and worked from the age of fourteen. And as we go further back in time, the younger children had to start work, to keep alive and help to make ends meet for them and their families.

My advice, to everyone is always being the best you can and make the most of your life. Do the things that you are able to and enjoy yourself. Remember more and more of us are clocking over eighty years on the life clock, we should not allow ourselves to be branded as `old fogies', just because we retire doesn't mean we are banished to the sofa , shuffling about in our zip up slippers and scanning the radio times for the repeat programs from our younger days. Remember, life is for living. Keeping your mind active is the real key to keeping going. A young mind keeps the old body going. Tell yourself. 'I'm not old, I'm like a fine wine that has matured and is too good to drink'

Nothing can be gained by worrying about the `Big D', when your time comes someone will come to take your soul home even if you're an atheist.

And God!

I do find it heartbreaking and sad when it is the death of someone who is young, it seems so unfair. I have been asked why? I can't tell them why. Life is life, but it is of no comfort to those who are grieving, remember that your loved one has gone home, and many will be reborn. How many people have you heard of who have a loved one die and a few months later have news of a new baby.

Children in the spirit world, who are not reborn straight away, carry on growing and have people who take care of them. This was a comfort to me, when my son Thomas came to see me from spirit world, he was now 21 years old, out of the blue, he just appeared by my bed and said he would take care of his little brother, I never saw him again.

Some religious beliefs can lead people to think they are being punished by God for something they have done. That is absolute rubbish. God does not punish you for your sins; it does not take your children away, or inflict sickness upon you. and so don't persist or blame yourself, life events happen for various reasons, so many in fact it is not possible to predict anything, as to who, what, where, when or why.

God often gets the blame when someone dies and yet we still carry out a service asking that their soul reaches heaven, committing the care of our loved ones to him.

I've been asked, 'Why did God let such a terrible thing happen?' 'Why didn't he stop it?' Life is not like that. He/she/ it does not choose, which person lives or dies, it is not a game of chess. This is, `LIFE', as we know it.

Think about it one minute we are blaming him/she/it etc for punishing us, then asking for help.

God didn't make war, disease or greed. Mankind has to accept responsibility for this. He gained knowledge, built complex societies, created religions; Mankind has killed maimed, raped and plundered, Often In the name of God. What a lame excuse for mans' greed, and his need to control others..

Mankind also ravaged Mother Earth, in his learning process, there was bound to be a price to pay, now Mother Earth is trying to rebalance. She absorbs negative energies and recycles them into positive ones, now even she is struggling and so we need to play our part. Carry out the right action and aid her healing. Think about how much negative comes from the actions of numerous wars and pollution over the centuries, that's just as a starting point.

Mother Earth has a lot of healing to do. Hence all the natural disasters we hear about every day, across the world. Give her as much love and support as you can if you want to do your bit.

Most of us on the spiritual path, don't view God as a man dishing out orders.

Some still refer to him and others her; originally it was goddesses who ruled in the early days, mother earth, gave birth to the crops and food that mankind needed. So the link with goddess was formed.

Some Indian and Buddhist belief systems have male gods
and female goddesses, each representing characteristics of men
and women's states of mind and the power they hold.
There is the balance of 'Ying and Yang,' female and male
energies. Everyone has both male and female energies within
them, this reflects in our character. For example a timid female
leans too much to the feminine side, 'Ying,' a stronger female
may be more dominant if she leans to the 'Yang' side.
When on the spiritual path you learn to recognise these
elements within you and become more of a balanced person.
The universal consciousness or God if you prefer is about love,
supporting us in our times on emotional, mental and spiritual
needs, and tolerance of each other; right action, peace, healing
of our world, and everything on it.
Mankind became disconnected from source so long ago, when
ego, power, greed, took over for so many years, As ancient
wisdom came to light in the form of scrolls and manuscripts,
written hundreds of years ago to help mankind, have been
buried, lost and hidden, misinterpreted rewritten and adapted
from writer to writer, incorporating their own point of view. If
you have ever played Chinese Whispers you will know what I
mean.
I feel we should not take ancient works, word for word; they
have been rewritten and reinterpreted, over and over again, so
many wars due to religion and belief's, personal interjections
of personal opinions. The basic essence contained in these
manuscripts was a guide of how we should live our lives; they
give what they saw at that time as the right actions we should
take. 'That time,' is the important point.
It is up to you to sort the chaff from the corn and make your
own decision as a child of the light.
For many years negativity has increased the hold on Mother
Earth, hence the balance of our planet tipped in the favor of
negative energies, and when I began this book in 2002 the

prospects for our future, looked dim. The powers that be knew this and decided something had to be done, and the balance readdressed. For many years more and more old souls have been reincarnated, from many realms. Remember the passage from the Bible, `My house has many mansions, those houses indicate I believe the realms of beings living within those houses so to speak, some are angelic, some old souls, some wise and ancient, some from other galaxies, and dimensions of time and space.

If you choose to work with spirit you will meet many beings and people who too have come to the service of mother earth and her people. All these beings have chosen to come back here to redress the balance, and some to take their brothers and sisters home. More people are awakening up to realise there is more to life, and this in turn brings in more positive energies. Many more old souls and spiritual people are working hard to make things change for the better. People are changing in a positive way and hearing that Mother Earth needs our help. As we look around the world positive things are happening and increasing.

There are those whose hearts seem hollow and don't care about the world. They are aware that there are problems and they just don't do anything about it, even though they know they could do something about it, and make positive changes. They make excuse after excuse to justify their lack of action.

Which one are you?

We are starting to take care of our planet, and appreciate what we have. As well as you and I, the rich and famous are also becoming aware that there is something else out there; there is more to life than we initially thought.

A whole dimension in time and space; which requires us to have an open heart and mind.

With love and care Mother Earth will bounce back, she
may look different from now, but the more positive changes
you can make the more positive energies will be available to
`All'
As for war, greed and inhumane acts that is down to Mankind
to sort out, with the support and the love of so many from those
higher realms how can we lose?
The door is open and it is up to us to grab the opportunity's
One and all…………. Ask for help from God, Goddess,
Angles, Spirits, etc., anyone who works for light and you can
be sure they will be champing at the bit to support you on your
campaign.

Nam myoho renge kyo

Mantra to release your highest potential

I wrote this book in a hope I would continue to help others by sharing my journeys of life's ups and downs, and to give you a glimpse of how the world of Spirit is so closely intertwined with our own, and also as an encouragement to you the reader, not just to explore the spiritual path but also to give you the confidence to make the most of your time on this plain. Enjoy and discover. Perhaps take a quick look back at something in your life that you started to learn, remember how new and how alien it was, perhaps even very difficult to grasp. Look at what you have achieved in your life maybe it's driving, or a college course, or even using a computer. Whatever was your challenge for you, to improve and develop? What is your life's dream? If you don't have dreams you can't make them come true.

You are an amazing human being and capable of far more than you think you are.

Are you thinking about having a go at something new? Or perhaps there is something you would like to do for no reason other than you have always fancied having a go, maybe dancing, singing, or climbing a mountain, playing an instrument, and the list goes on.

Whatever it may be, why not have a go? Life is an adventure, what stops you living it? If there are things that stop you, look for another way, or another dream.

Have a little book and on each page write something you would like to do, own, or play, perhaps somewhere you would like to go. I call it my do before I die list; there are all sorts of things in mine, from going to see the opera, or a real orchestra, seeing a west end show. I always wanted to waltz around a ballroom floor in a beautiful dress, with the man of my dreams, owning a Native American flute, meeting people like the elders of ancient tribes, owning a Volkswagen camper van, a blue one with white flowers on. I can't waltz, I don't think my arthritis would let me drive a camper van, the people I want to meet are spread all over the world, there are so many obstacles to reaching my dreams............However, I will still have a go regardless. Our state of mind and determination is a remover of obstacles, you would be surprised at how many you can achieve and will come to pass, so write it down, and create your reality. Also think positively; negative energy attracts negative, remember. No matter how gloomy things seem think positive, and it will attract positive and things will turn in you favor.

There is a whole new world waiting to be explored within the 'Realms of Light' And where am I now seventeen years down the line from that first meeting with Mary. Well my lessons are ongoing, classes in Angels and higher orders, Sanskrit mantra, development, self-healing, shamanic sound, giving out keys to those who want them, and as I finish this last chapter, I start to prepare to give a new set of keys were this part of my journey first began, a stranger in a set of four dreams eighteen years ago, A man in black I had never heard of, who I now know was the key to my new adventure in sacred sound.

The main hall is booked and the third staged event delivering the world of sound healing in a new format, it is exciting, I have childlike wonder, and the p word patience of the adult mind, With the Spirit words that fill my head with new ideas and inspiration, words of the new books, tumble on the computer screen, songs and music that whizz around in my head.

The groups and classes! All those that have worked within the groups, have grown beyond their belief and it is time for those chicks to leave the nest and fly in their own direction.

As I set about raising new chicks, however only temporary, the seasoned hens and cockerels look at advancing their energies and commit to world service with the world of sound vibrations and higher energy's,
Spirit tell me I'm going away, traveling and for someone who gets travel sick on a garden swing it's a scary prospect, they don't say where or when I will go.
I have grown and will continue to grow, I look forward to new lessons and the new adventure, the year of 2011 began with a very bleak outlook. However, I kept my faith and strength in their world.
I'm still here, at the tender age of fifty four, I don't focus on the aches and pains of maturity or ill health, the love handles, cellulite, and wrinkles, or life's worries, like a map that shows where you have been, only you can make the changes to where you will go, no matter how small a step or how tentative
What have you got to lose by trying?
You are reading my story right now, so you have all already made a conscious or subconscious decision to make changes to yourself and play your part in saving Mother Earth...improving your life and growing to your full potential.
Maybe you thought the book was all rubbish, and yet you read it, so your mind is open: Good, that is all I ask of you.

And now my friend the teapots empty and we have eaten all the shortbread biscuits, so it is time for me to leave you now.
I hope I have at least given you one key to open a door to something better, spiritually or in your life it doesn't really matter, you have grown by just reading the beginning of my adventure, and will continue to do so as you walk the track in your adventure.
I put on my spiritual back pack now, full of my life's lessons, experiences, all the tears, joy, the endings and beginnings the tools, that I have shared with you so far, I start the next part of

my adventure, and I look forward to another chat on my return,

The last words of this final draft in August 2014 of 'The Phoenix within' is written from my new home, a narrow boat in the middle of Nottingham city, spirit said I would travel, and after moving up and down the canal and a brief stay in the marina over the last seventeen months, I have very itchy feet, I can barely cruse my boat and discovered the fifty seven foot boat I purchased is in fact sixty foot long, this size boat, I was told not to buy and that I would never handle her alone, She is my home and I love her, so I will succeed in cruising her proficiently even with the odds stacked again me, I'm looking to continue my adventure on the British water ways, …for someone who doesn't like deep water and gets sick on a swing who would have thought it, another adventure for another book……life's for living…..live it well'

'THE TIME HAS COME …….THE TIME IS NOW'
(Tim Wheater Heartland)